21 DAYS TO
OVER
FLOW

Your life will never be the same!

21 DAYS TO
OVER
FLOW

A DEVOTIONAL TO BRING SPIRITUAL RESTORATION AND HEAVENLY FIRE

BY

JEREMIAH HOSFORD

ZECHARIAH MINISTRIES INTERNATIONAL

FOREWORD

If you are ready to experience God at a greater level than you even thought possible then get this book! It truly is a hand-book to personal and corporate awakening.

As I read *21 Days to Overflow* by my friend Pastor and Author Jeremiah Hosford, I personally realized that I needed a course correction. My busyness had caused me to begin to hold my breath and not experience the breath of God. It is time to breathe once again. As a child of the King you deserve to experience the breath of God. Job 33:4 says, *"The Spirit of God has made me; the breath of the Almighty gives me life."* You see not only do I know and trust the author, but I have leaned on him many times for wisdom and refreshing. So, as I read this book my spirit experienced what can only be described as a Psalm 42:7, *"deep cries to deep . . . "* moment of awakening.

I challenge you to join me and take the *21 Days to Overflow* journey. If you do though, I must warn you that you will soon realize that your 'normal' way of doing life, simply will not do anymore! In fact, it is possible that your life will change drastically. This book will awaken you to the fact that lethargy and monotony, in life, can only be interrupted by the indwelling and breath of God. You will no longer be able to settle for milk and not meat (Hebrews 5:12) in your daily approach to God. Pastor Jeremiah shows us that we are called first to be emptied of all that corrupts our lives and keeps us from being free. Most Christians never experience what it is like to completely die to self. Why? Because somewhere along the way life and experiences has robbed each of us of understanding that *"For to me, to live is Christ and to die is gain (Phil. 1:21)"* Once you are empty then God can fill you up with His Spirit, purpose and power! This is the moment you will abdicate your personal thrown to worship at the Kings feet. What you will begin to realize is that it is simultaneous. What do I mean? You will have the James 4:8 encounter, *"Come near to God and he will come near to you. Wash your hands, you sinners, and purify your hearts, you double-minded."* You are called to mobile-upper-room. God will invade your life andsimultaneously, each day as you read, pray and fast you will become keenly aware that you are called to be *"the righteousness of God (2 Cor. 5:21)."* As his messengers of hope and freedom you will soon understand that this means you are the "overflow" of God's power, love and freedom.

I am so blessed that my friend has written this book. It has personally set me ablaze with a passion for more of Jesus and a hunger than can only be filled in His presence. Generations from now will point to this book as the kindling that was lit to help bring revival-fire to a church and people that are ready for authentic encounters that lead to the power and demonstration of a mighty God. I believe that as Pastor Jeremiah said, "The days of Heavenly-Fire" are truly upon us. So, let us not dare miss our moment!

Evangelist & Author Pat Schatzline
Remnant Ministries International
Author of "Restore the Roar" & "Rebuilding the Altar"
www.raisetheremnant.com

INTRODUCTION

over·flow \ ,ō-var-'flō \

intransitive verb

1 : to flow over bounds
2 : to fill a space to capacity and spread beyond its limits
(Merriam-Webster Dictionary)

OVERFLOW

I never realized the implications that one word could have. I did not realize that a word that first took root in my spirit, and then was declared over my congregation would have such an effect that it would transform the way we would think and act. I had no idea that it would revolutionize our prayer life, our worship, our leadership, our planning, our calendar—virtually everything. I don't think I could have anticipated the new opportunities that arose, as well as the things that would be left in our rearview mirror. I would find myself pleasantly surprised by the relationships it would repair. I would also be surprised that some would choose not to walk in it, and that it would put distance between us and them. I did not realize the fear that this word would strike in the realms of hell, and the darkness that we would have to fight. I could not have anticipated that this would result in some of the greatest victories we would ever witness.

All I knew was, as the year 2017 came to a close, that God had spoken to us and said that 2018 would be a year of overflow. As we sought Him, He gave us a clear path to this life of overflow. This path, the very one laid out here, has been the launching pad for a spiritual, physical, emotional, relational, and financial life that we seemed to have merely tasted before.

The Holy Spirit prepared us for this process by helping us understand where we were starting. We were unable to walk in this full life of overflow because we were so full of ourselves. Before we could begin to know about this life of spiritual restoration and heavenly fire, we had to move ourselves out of the way. As the Spirit began to reveal to us that we were starting this process full of us, we first needed to allow Him to empty us of ourselves. However, to be empty of ourselves would do us no good, if we were not filled with the Holy Spirit. So, the next thing we had to seek was a fresh infilling of the Spirit. Then, and only then, we would be prepared to receive this overflowing life.

Because you are holding this book, you are preparing to walk this path into this incredible overflowing life. Indeed, you have already begun. There is a longing in the deepest part of who you are that says there is more out there for you. You have a belief that you serve a big God, and that He does big things for those who put their trust in Him. You possess a keen awareness that there is a deeper depth, a greater breakthrough, a more abundant life, a higher knowledge, a hopeful hope, a joyful joy, a peace that surpasses anything you can understand, and a heavenly fire that will refine everything it touches.

As we began this process, we knew it had to be coupled with fasting and prayer. From day one, we fasted sunup to sundown (6:00 AM-6:00 PM). We doubled the number of our corporate prayer times and opened our church facilities all day to accommodate those who would want to come and pray throughout the day, in addition to increasing the fervor of our own personal prayer lives. If you are able to, I encourage you to add fasting and prayer to your journey to this overflowing life as well. If you have a spouse, family member, good friend, mentor—anyone—who could walk this with you—even better.

Whatever your approach, get ready to step into a greater realm of spiritual restoration and heavenly fire! Get ready for the overflow!

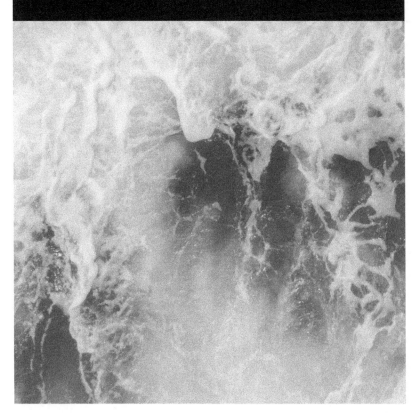

WEEK ONE
EMPTY ME

DAY ONE
WORLDLINESS

Do not love the world or the things in the world.
If anyone loves the world, the love of the Father is not in him.
For all that is in the world—the lust of the flesh, the lust of the
eyes, and the pride of life—is not of the Father but is of the world.
And the world is passing away, and the lust of it; but he who
does the will of God abides forever.

Little children, it is the last hour; and as you have heard that
the Antichrist is coming, even now many antichrists have come,
by which we know that it is the last hour. They went out
from us, but they were not of us; for if they had been of us,
they would have continued with us; but they went out that they
might be made manifest, that none of them were of us.

But you have an anointing from the Holy One,
and you know all things.
1 John 2:15-20

We are beginning this journey to empty us of us. The Bible is telling us, as followers of Christ, those who have been bought with the blood of Jesus, who are filled with the Spirit, that we are not to love the things of this world. I know this is a stark contrast to many of the things being taught today, but we must know that, as followers of Christ, we are to deny ourselves, take up our cross, and follow Jesus.

The apostle Paul tells us in Romans 12 that we are not to be conformed to the pattern of this world, but we are to be transformed by the renewing of our minds, that we may prove the good, acceptable, and perfect will of God. This word *renewing* comes from the Greek word, *anakainōsis,* which means to renovate. In this context, it means we are to get rid of all of our old worldly ways of thinking, acting, and living, and begin to replace these with the things of God.

As we enter this time of prayer and fasting, we must begin by asking the Lord, "What worldly mindsets, attitudes, and behaviors do I have in me? What is in me that is keeping me from going forward in You?"

When you ask God this question, you will find that the Holy Spirit will put His finger on these areas of your life, and expose them. When He does this, don't resist Him, because this is the beginning of the process of Him emptying you of you. This makes room for Him to fill you with more of His power, presence, and love.

We are to be vessels of God, shining His light in the earth. The Bible tells us in Matthew chapter five that we are the salt of the earth, the light of the world—a city that is set on a hill that cannot be hidden.

> *For all that is in the world—the lust of the flesh,*
> *the lust of the eyes, and the pride of life—*
> *is not of the Father but is of the world.*
> *1 John 2:16*

All sin falls under these three categories. We can follow it back to the Garden of Eden. When Adam and Eve fell into sin, the lust of the flesh, the lust of the eyes, and the pride of life were all there.

Satan does not have any new tactics. He only presents the same old stuff in a new wrapping. Every temptation that comes into your life will involve one or more of these three. We are not to give into any of these things, but instead we must lean on the power of the Holy Spirit. He will convict us. He will warn us. He will empower us. He will give us grace—not as license to sin, but to keep us from sin.

And the world is passing away, and the lust of it;
but he who does the will of God abides forever.
1 John 2:17

This means that if our love is with the world, and in the things of the world, we are going to pass away with this world. However, if our love, passion, and heart are with God and in God, then we won't pass away with this world. We have a promise of eternal life with Him, in heaven.

Today, I am inviting you to pray a dangerous prayer. It is a prayer that is dangerous to our flesh, but awesome for our spirit. This prayer will ignite the power of the Holy Spirit in your life, and allow Him to begin the work of emptying you of your worldly desires, so you can be filled with more of Him.

Let's pray this together. . .

Father, in the name of Jesus, I ask you through the leading, power, and fellowship of the Holy Spirit, that you will reveal to me any and all worldliness that may be in me.

I repent of this worldliness. I repent of the attitudes and behaviors it produces in my life. I repent of selfishness.

I ask that you would fill those places with Jesus. Manifest the presence of God in me, on me, and through me. Allow me to sense the same power that raised Jesus from the grave. Do this for Your name's sake. Do this for Your glory. Do this for Your Kingdom to advance in this earth. Let it manifest on me so powerfully that I may sense the infilling of your Spirit in my body, mind, and spirit.

I ask this in Jesus' name. Amen.

I encourage you to pray this prayer throughout the day. Each time the Holy Spirit reveals something to you, repent and allow Him to remove the worldly things from your life and fill those empty places with Him. I believe that you will even experience healing in your physical body as freedom from these things comes into your life.

ASK YOURSELF

- What is in my life that keeps me from God?

- What areas of my life have been kept back from God?

- What worldly mindsets does God want to free me from?

DAY TWO
DISTRACTIONS

Finally, brethren, whatever things are true, whatever things are noble, whatever things are just, whatever things are pure, whatever things are lovely, whatever things are of good report, if there is any virtue and if there is anything praiseworthy— meditate on these things.
Philippians 4:8

A lot of the things that distract and hinder us are things that run through our minds on a constant basis. When we are struggling in a season of life, when we can't seem to find peace, and our lives are in disarray, it is often because there is so much bombarding our minds. When this happens, we have to begin to take control over our thoughts. We have to apprehend the thoughts that are causing the distractions, hindrances, and struggles and put them out of our minds and our lives.

Though we cannot control every thought that comes into our minds, we can control how we respond to them. When we entertain thoughts, we give them an audience. We cannot permit ourselves to give an audience to worldly thoughts—thoughts that come straight from hell. We have to drive those thoughts from our minds, and instead meditate on the truth. Deception is running rampant through the world, and sometimes even the church. We have to meditate on what is true, noble, just, pure, lovely, of good report, virtuous, and praiseworthy.

Just imagine if social media could only tell the truth. What kind of different world would we live in, if only this one avenue of communication could only reveal truth? Now, imagine if every thought you entertained was the truth. Imagine how much more wonderful your life would be.

Sometimes, the worst part of deception is that we don't realize we are being deceived. The lies come on in layers, and eventually become so thick that the truth sounds like a lie. This is what is happening in the world today. It's hard for people to comprehend the gospel when it is heard, because of the prevailing lies. Many in the church have become deceived because they have bought into the lies of the world. The world can never define truth. John 17:17 says, "Your word is truth." Anything that disagrees with the Word of God is a lie. Paul says it like this, in Romans 3:4, "Let God be true but every man a liar." When we come to the place that our thinking and our behavior, or even the way we feel, disagrees with what the Word of God says, we are wrong. The Word is not.

Have you ever thought about how addicted we are to negativity? We have an almost insatiable hunger for a bad report. We will skip over, scroll past, and change the channel of things that are good and positive, so we can entertain things that are negative. We have to get our hearts and minds to the place that we are no longer addicted to a negative report.

Ask yourself this question as you go through your day: "Are my thoughts praiseworthy?" If the answer to this question is no, you must push that thought out of your mind, and shift your focus to thoughts that are praiseworthy. This is very challenging, and will seem like battle for days, maybe even longer. However, in time you will begin to gain victory in your mind. This is the beginning of our gaining the ability to discern between that which is holy, and that which is not. When we remove these distractions from our lives, we can get back to the place where we can hear God's voice.

You may find yourself in a place that you no longer sense God's presence, even if you love the Lord, and you are faithful to attend church, because of all the distractions in your life. You have not felt the communion and fellowship of the Holy Spirit in a long time. You have not been in the secret place with God in a long time. You have been going through the motions of being a believer, but you have not been alone with the Lord in a long time. You are so distracted that you cannot hear His voice anymore.

The prayer you are about to pray is going to be dangerous to your flesh, but helpful to your spirit. You are going to ask God to reveal and remove all distractions from your life. After you pray this prayer, God will begin to speak to you and let you know the things that do not belong in your life. Then, it is up to you to release those things, even if it is painful to let them go. If you don't do this, and you allow the distractions to persist, you will get to a place where you will not be able to hear God when He speaks.

Let's pray this together. . .

Father, in the name of Jesus, I ask You to show me any and all distractions in my life. I ask you, Holy Spirit, to remove them. I ask You to fill me with more of You. Empty me of me. Fill me with You. I ask this in Jesus' name. Amen.

ASK YOURSELF

- What things do I often find myself meditating on?

- What most distracts my mind from meditating on God's word?

- What lies from the enemy do I find myself being told?

DAY THREE
DECEPTIONS

Beloved, do not believe every spirit, but test the spirits,
whether they are of God; because many false prophets have
gone out into the world.
1 John 4:1

Just because something speaks, no matter whether it shouts or whispers, does not mean that it is the Spirit of God. Just because we feel led to do a thing doesn't mean it is the right thing.

As we have said before, there are many who love God, and go to church regularly, but are deceived. As people of God, we have forgotten that we have an obligation to test the spirits. Every voice, every leading must be tested with the Word of God. We have to test every spirit. Especially in this day and time.

There is a false gospel being preached right now that says that God doesn't require anything of you. This gospel says you can live any way you want to, with no standard of holiness. This gospel is even being promoted from some pulpits by men and women who are called to preach. The Bible tells us in 1 Peter 1:16, "Be holy, for I am holy." Hebrews 12:14 says, "Pursue peace with all people, and holiness, without which no one will see the Lord." We must hold everything we hear in the light of God's Word, and if it doesn't line up, it is a lie.

One of the times we must test what kind of spirit we are hearing is when we leave churches. I understand there are times when

God calls us to leave. When we pray and fast, and feel the leading of the Lord to go, we go to our pastor and let them know that we feel the leading to leave, and that we want to do it in the right way. Our desire is to go with blessing and celebration and not leave in a bad or negative way. However, these types of exits are the overwhelming minority of cases when people choose to leave their church. Most often people get offended, hurt, mad, or begin to disagree with someone, and actually let themselves believe that this is God speaking to them about leaving their church.

There are times that a spirit will tell us to get a divorce from our mate, and get together with another person we are attracted to. There are spirits that tell us to do all sorts of things, from all sorts of motivations. We must test the spirits to see if they are of God or not. If the spirit that is speaking is from God, follow it, but if it is not from God, we must rebuke that spirit and tell it to go from our lives.

There are times we will hear some voice, from without or within, and we never test the spirit to see if it is from God. We know this is something that Jesus prophesied about the church of the last days. As He began His teaching to His disciples regarding the signs of the end times, He said, "Take heed that you not be deceived." Why? Because in the end times, deception will run rampant.

Is there a voice inside you, whether you listen to it or not, that lets you know that what you are doing or thinking is wrong, even when you don't want to hear it? This is the voice of the Holy Spirit inside you. If you hear this, the Holy Spirit is doing His work on the inside of you. Can you hear the voice of the Holy Spirit?

Do not be deceived, God is not mocked; for whatever
a man sows, that he will also reap. For he who sows to his flesh
will of the flesh reap corruption, but he who sows to the
Spirit will of the Spirit reap everlasting life.
Galatians 6:7-8

God does not want us to be deceived. He wants us walking in the truth. However, it is the truth that we know that will make us free. There are times that the enemy causes us to look at truth as if it is bondage. I believe this is the case with many who have taken up this devotional. I believe that the enemy has lied to you and told you that the Christian life is a life of bondage.

Just as Satan did with Adam and Eve in the garden, he tries to pull our eyes off all the things that are available to us, including everlasting abundant life, to make us focus on the one thing that is off-limits. He tries to get us to focus on what we don't need to do, instead of the things we can do. He tries to make us believe that God keeping us from destructive things is bondage. However, the reality is that deception will never make us free.

When we obey the Lord, in truth, freedom comes, deliverance comes, power comes, peace comes, love comes, compassion comes—everything that flows down from the Father of Lights flows down into our lives.

We must ask the Holy Spirit to reveal any and all deceptions that may be in our lives, and are coming against our minds. We must ask God to forgive us for allowing these things to be considered truth in our lives.

Pray this prayer with me. . .

Father, in the name of Jesus, I ask that Your Holy Spirit would reveal any and every deception that is in my life, and that is coming against my mind. I ask You to forgive me for allowing them to become even a consideration of truth. I ask you to bring down the walls of deception in my life. Bring down the mindsets that have tried to exalt themselves above the Word of God. I ask that you would begin to silence the voice of the enemy. I ask that the voice of the Holy Spirit would begin to reverberate down to the very depths of my soul. I ask that the voice of the Spirit, and the Word of God would begin to be so clear to me that I would be able to immediately to discern between Your voice and the enemy's. Let me no longer be led by deception, but let me be led by truth, and let this truth I know make me free.

I plead the blood of Jesus over my mind, and I command any chains of deception to be destroyed in the name of Jesus. I break every tie to the lies of Satan off my life right now. I release the truth of God, the power of the Holy Spirit, and the anointing that destroys every yoke of bondage right now in the name of Jesus.

I thank you for doing this. I ask all these things in the mighty name of Jesus. Amen.

(One more thing, before we go. If you are away from the church, you need to get back in. If you are in a church that is preaching deception, you need to get out and find one that preaches the truth. You must get to a place where the Spirit of God is moving and where you cannot attend week after week and stay comfortable in your sin.)

ASK YOURSELF

- How can I prevent deception in my life?

- What are some areas in my life where I need to test the spirits?

- Is my focus more on what God has offered me, or on what Satan wants me to consider "off-limits"?

DAY FOUR
SELFISHNESS

Let nothing be done through selfish ambition or conceit,
but in lowliness of mind let each esteem others better than
himself. Let each of you look out not only for his own interests,
but also for the interests of others.
Philippians 2:3-4

What we do, not just in church, but outside of church cannot be done with a spirit of selfish ambition or conceit. Whether we are at work, at school, with friends, with family, in the market-place, or serving in our place of leadership, our motives matter.

Sadly, we have all been witness to the fact that the church has become selfish. We have situations where pastors are having to strategize to get their services condensed into fifty minutes, because people just won't make the time to spend in the house of God. People of God, is fifty minutes all we really have for the Lord? Do we not realize that the time we have, the body we have—the very life we have—is not our own? It has been bought and paid for with the blood of Jesus Christ. Therefore, nothing we do can be done in selfishness or conceit.

The question we should be asking ourselves is not, "What is best for me?" Instead, we should be asking ourselves, "What is best for the Kingdom of God?" Our ambition should be to find the best way to do the perfect will of God.

Our scripture today tells us that what we do should be done in lowliness of mind. This means that we are not prideful, arrogant, or puffed up. We never try to put ourselves above others, but we do as the Bible says in 1 Peter 5:6: Humble ourselves under the mighty hand of God, that He may exalt us in due time.

It also tells us that we esteem our brothers and sisters above ourselves. This means we are not tearing them down, but we are strengthening them. We're not gossiping about our brothers and sisters in Christ, even under the guise of a "prayer group." Instead, we are encouraging them and helping them. We are not jealous when they are doing well. We are happy and celebrate when they succeed. We are not leaving them on their own when they are down. We are helping them. As Romans 12:15 says, we "rejoice with those who rejoice, and weep with those who weep."

When we put others before ourselves, the Holy Spirit does a powerful work in our lives. I am a firm believer in what you make happen for others, God will make happen for you. We must have our heart in such a place that we *want* to help someone else. We must want God to use us to make things happen for others, even if we receive no recognition for it.

You may have fallen prey to this trap of the enemy, and left your church because you did not feel like you were adequately recognized for the things you did. You felt overlooked and overworked, and because people did not stop to say, "Thank you . . . I appreciate you," you stopped in the middle of your call. I'm not saying that it is right for people to go unappreciated. However, you cannot let the shortcomings of others stop what God is doing through you.

If you are in this spot, you need to stop and repent right now, and go forward with the realization that everything you are doing is unto the Lord, and not unto men. So even if they never say "Thank you," one day, God will. As soon as you repent, you will feel the call of God reignite in your life again. You will have passion and the presence of God overflowing in your life once again.

When we do as the scripture says and not only look out for our own interest, but for the interests of others, we will see the situations in the lives of our brothers and sisters in a whole new light. When we see them hurting, struggling, in despair, or in need, and we are in a place to help them, we should. This could be as simple as hugging them and letting them know we are praying for them, and that we have their back.

When we do this, the selfish ambition in us that we didn't even know existed will be exposed. We will also find that our days of minding someone else's business will end. So often, we get so caught up in what everyone else is doing that we fail to have our own stuff together. The Bible has nothing good to say about busybodies.

The next time we attempt to do anything for others, or for the Lord, let's ask Him to reveal if our motivation is selfish. I declare this over you: this will begin to uncover wells in your life. Places of provision and refreshing that have been clogged up will be uncovered. You will begin to drink from these wells again. You will sense the Spirit of God anoint you, put life back into you, put fire back in you, and put passion back into you. Doors of opportunity will open for you because you have repented of selfishness and have invited the Lord to take over every area of your life.

We will begin this today with our prayer.

Father, in the name of Jesus, I ask the Holy Spirit to reveal any and all selfishness in thought, deed, time, talent, and treasure. Father, I repent of this and ask Your forgiveness. I make a fresh commitment to You in every area of my life today.

I ask, Father, that You would come in and stir me in such a way that every part of my life would be completely devoted to You. I ask you to be first in thought, deed, time, talent, and treasure— every area of my life. Holy Spirit, manifest Yourself in my life. Fill me with love and compassion, from this day forward. Let me be busy about my Father's business. As I seek Your face, let the heavens open over my life. Let me hear You and be guided by You.

Father, I thank You for doing this. I ask all of these things in Jesus' name. Amen.

ASK YOURSELF

- What areas of my life do I consider selfless?

- What areas of my life do I consider selfish?

- Do I believe that what I make happen for others that God will make happen for me? Why or why not?

- What are practical ways I can begin to put God first in my life?

DAY FIVE
PRIDE

But He gives more grace. Therefore He says:

"God resists the proud,
But gives grace to the humble."
Therefore submit to God. Resist the devil and he will flee
from you. Draw near to God and He will draw near to you.
Cleanse your hands, you sinners; and purify your hearts,
you double-minded.
James 4:6-8

We have made it to the fifth day of emptying us of us. This has not been easy!

Picture this. You get a clean glass from the cupboard. You fill just the bottom part of it with muddy water; then you fill it the rest of the way with clean water. No matter how much clean water you add, the residue of the dirty water will still be there and contaminate the clean water you add.

So often, we ask Jesus to fill us with more of Him, but we still have the "muddy water" of sin and flesh in us, and the contamination prevents us from experiencing the presence of God in His fullness. We subject ourselves to this painful process of emptying ourselves of the corruption of our flesh, so the fresh outpouring from God in our lives is undefiled.

No one likes to admit that they struggle with pride. King

Saul of the Old Testament had a calling, an anointing, talents, and abilities, but he allowed compromise to come into his life. In his attempt to justify it, he gave way to the sin of pride.

However, before he ever became king, we get a peek into the kind of person he was, when the prophet Samuel had to bring correction for his disobedience and pride.

So Samuel said, "When you were little in your own eyes, were you not head of the tribes of Israel? And did not the Lord anoint you king over Israel?"
1 Samuel 15:17

Just like it did with King Saul, pride has a way of entering our lives with subtlety. In the same way it masqueraded itself in King Saul, pride often disguises itself as false humility. False humility is not Biblical humility. Biblical humility is proven in the private place. It is rewarded in the public place. However, false humility reveals itself as pride in the place where we are alone. God judged King Saul, because He saw the heart of King Saul.

How many times has God asked us to do something, and we have either not done it, or we have done it halfway? This is pride. This is us saying, "I am God, and I know what's best for me in this situation."

We struggle with this when it comes to things like family, work, and particularly finances. We are called upon to obey God in the tithe and in offerings, but our pride gets in the way of this, and ultimately keeps us from experiencing the blessings of God.

God not only wants our obedience, He wants us to do it His way. Why? Because His ways are perfect, and ours are not.

He resists the proud. Think about that. He resists the proud. This means He holds the proud far off, but He gives grace to the humble.

Every day, we need grace. We need the power of the Holy Spirit to live a holy life. We need the power of the Holy Spirit to keep us from doing the things our flesh wants to do. We need the power of the Holy Spirit so we can continue to walk in the call of God. In the times when we fall short, and we repent, we need the grace of God to cover us and cleanse us. The only way for us to receive this grace is to clothe ourselves in humility. Our mind, our hearts, our spirits must be clothed with humility.

> *Pride goes before destruction,*
> *And a haughty spirit before a fall.*
> *Proverbs 16:18*

I have witnessed pride in marriages, as one spouse refused to humble themselves, and it brought destruction to the family. I've seen it in the call of God on people's lives, as God brought them success in ministry, and because of this success, their heart was lifted up and pride began to sneak in, and destruction came. Sooner or later, pride will take you down. It will bring you to a place you never intended to be. It will bring destruction in your life.

> *Humble yourselves in the sight of the Lord,*
> *and He will lift you up.*
> *James 4:10*

Today, we have to pray and humble ourselves. When we truly humble ourselves, the Lord will forgive us and continue to use us. We must ask God to keep us little in our own eyes.

Pray this prayer with me.

Father, in Jesus' name, I ask you to forgive me of any and all pride. I repent of all pride that I know of, and that which I do not know of. I ask you, Holy Spirit, to help me to stay humble, to stay small in my own eyes, and to clothe me with humility.

Help me, God. Keep my heart soft. Keep my mind yielded. Keep my heart sensitive to Your presence. In Jesus' name I ask this. Amen.

ASK YOURSELF

- What are some "muddy-waters" God is revealing to me about my life?

- How can these be cleansed?

- How can I begin to use Biblical humility in my life?

DAY SIX
OFFENSE

He who covers a transgression seeks love,
But he who repeats a matter separates friends.
Proverbs 17:9

Here we are on Day Six. We have had to tackle some pretty difficult subjects over the past few days. It is no small thing to empty me of me. However, I want to assure you, the Holy Spirit is shouting over your life right now. I know your flesh is screaming, but your spirit is shouting too. Be encouraged today. You are growing stronger, even if it does not feel that way just now. Keep the faith. Persevere. Your life is being transformed. Distractions are being bound, as anointing is being released in your life.

Now, let's dive into the Word of God.

Offense is one of the most effective tools Satan uses in his campaign to hinder the people of God. He brings down even the mightiest of people. He uses offense to keep the Kingdom of God from being its most effective. He uses offense to dismantle churches. He uses offense to tear families apart. He uses offense to divide believers. He uses offense to perpetuate emotional, mental, and even physical illness in people.

Then [Jesus] said to the disciples,
"It is impossible that no offenses should come,
but woe to him through whom they do come!"
Luke 17:1

The question is not whether you will be offended; it is when will you be offended. Jesus tells us that it is *impossible* that no offense will come. It will come. What we do with offense, when it arrives, will tell us everything about our how our destiny will be fulfilled.

Pursue peace with all people, and holiness, without which
no one will see the Lord: looking carefully lest anyone fall short
of the grace of God; lest any root of bitterness springing
up cause trouble, and by this many become defiled;
Hebrews 12:14-15

How does a root of bitterness grow in a person? It comes when we get offended and respond incorrectly. As we see from our scripture readings in both Proverbs and Hebrews, the correct response to offense is to make peace with the offender or the offended. A dear minister friend of mine once told me, the root of bitterness cannot grow in the soil of forgiveness. When the ground of our hearts contains the soil of forgiveness, bitterness will die.

A root of bitterness doesn't automatically exist. It is not something we are born with. The writer of Hebrews tells us that it *springs* up, *causes* trouble, and by it many *become* defiled. A root of bitterness only gains its existence when we allow offense to spoil the fruitful ground of our lives. Sadly, I have observed dedicated, passionate, serving, tenderhearted Christians develop a root of bitterness in their lives, all because something came along, caused offense, and they responded to it with unforgiveness.

To be sure, the offenses in many cases were blatant wrongs done against these people. Wrong things happened. Something was said wrong. Something was done wrong. They were lied to. They were falsely accused. They were cheated or cheated on. They were gossiped about. They were treated unfairly. Friendships were lost. Ministries got all tangled up in lies, politics, accusations, jealousies, and other unholy things. However, when these things were not properly dealt with, the root of bitterness sprang up, and these dedicated Christians became polluted, and the once fruitful lives they lived became toxic. This is what happens when we allow offense to go undealt with.

You will know them by their fruits. Do men gather grapes from thornbushes or figs from thistles? Even so, every good tree bears good fruit, but a bad tree bears bad fruit. A good tree cannot bear bad fruit, nor can a bad tree bear good fruit. Every tree that does not bear good fruit is cut down and thrown into the fire. Therefore by their fruits you will know them.
Matthew 7:16-20

Like a pristine, fertile piece of land that becomes a dumping ground, when our lives accumulate more and more trash, it begins to spoil what was once productive. Jesus tells us that we will know who a person is by the kind of fruit they produce. A healthy spirit produces healthy fruit. A toxic spirit produces toxic fruit.

Have you found yourself struggling to produce good fruit in your life? Have you wrestled with quitting ministry because the passion has been choked out by bitterness and offense? Do you find it a struggle to go to church, fellowship with other believers, and worship God? Has your hunger for God's Word and prayer been replaced by a hunger for things of this world? If so, there is a root of bitterness in you.

However, I have good news. The Holy Spirit has come to remove this from your life. A fleet of dump trucks have come into your life, are being filled up with the garbage that has accumulated, and are hauling it away. As the last truck leaves with the last of the trash, here comes another fleet of trucks, loaded down with the most fertile new soil, ready to lay new ground in your life. This is what is about to happen to you, by the power of the Holy Spirit. I know you couldn't help what has been done to you, but you can help how you respond. Today, we are going to respond to this in a Biblical way.

Will you pray this prayer with me today?

Father, in Jesus' name, I ask You to forgive me of any and all offense that I may have in my heart toward anyone or anything. Today, I repent of all bitterness, all anger, all hatred, and all malice. Holy Spirit, I ask You to pull up any root of bitterness that I have allowed into the soil of my heart. I ask You to keep me humble and keep me forgiving. Whenever offense comes, and I am tempted to be unforgiving, please remind me that Christ Jesus freely forgave me. Let me be quick to forgive, and slow to anger, in Jesus' name I pray. Amen.

ASK YOURSELF

- How have I been offended? How did I respond to the offense?

- What did I learn from my experience of being offended and my response?

- Moving forward, how will I respond to offense differently?

DAY SEVEN
UNFORGIVENESS

"For if you forgive men their trespasses, your heavenly Father will also forgive you. But if you do not forgive men their trespasses, neither will your Father forgive your trespasses."
Matthew 6:14-15

Yesterday, we began to talk about the subjects of forgiveness and unforgiveness as they pertained to offense. In our final day of emptying us of us, I believe it is absolutely necessary that we deal with unforgiveness head-on.

Unforgiveness is wicked. It is spiritually, emotionally, and physically destructive. It takes and takes, and gives nothing in return. What's more, we see from today's scripture that our forgiveness from God is contingent upon our forgiving others. Eternity, literally heaven and hell, hangs in the balance of our willingness to forgive. The destiny of our souls rests on our decision to forgive, or not forgive, one another.

Every time I preach and make this statement, I feel people saying, "Pastor, you don't know what they did." And they are right. I can't know the hurt. I can't imagine the depth of the scars that are left in the wake of their mistreatment. I know that things happen that only the victim and the victimizer know about.

One thing I do know. The longer you allow unforgiveness to fester in your heart, the more you will find a false security in holding onto it. The longer you hold onto it, the harder it will be to let it go.

When I pray for people for physical healing, I always ask them if they are harboring any unforgiveness in their hearts. I have seen for myself, and heard from others, stories of people debilitated by physical illnesses, because they were clinging to unforgiveness. I am aware of a man who went into the hospital with a tremendous physical illness. The doctors were testing for every kind of illness, all to no avail. The source of his sickness could not be determined. After a time in the hospital, this man forgave a person he had held a grudge against for a very long time. Within five days, he left the hospital totally healed. Unforgiveness keeps us from receiving the fullness of what God has for us.

Every time I am tempted to harbor unforgiveness, I think about what my forgiveness cost Jesus. When I think about what it might cost me to let the person go, I have to remember that it cost Jesus His life. It cost my Lord everything so I might be forgiven. When I compare my tiny losses, pride, making of amends, or whatever it might take, with the loss of His life, it makes the decision to forgive so much easier.

Understand this: we are not forgiving others for them. We are forgiving them for us. Our lack of forgiving a person doesn't keep them chained. It keeps us chained. There is a freedom that comes when we forgive. As we pray today, the chains that fall will be falling from us. Even if people never forgive us, it doesn't matter. We will be free. We will be made right with God.

Let's pray this prayer together. . .

Father, in Jesus' name, I ask You to show any unforgiveness that I may hold against anyone. Show me anyone, in my world, or in the church, that I have not forgiven.

I repent of unforgiveness I have held in my heart. I forgive everyone who has hurt me, and I ask that you, Heavenly Father, would forgive them too. Bless them, I pray, in the name of Jesus.

Holy Spirit, this day I officially release them from any chains of unforgiveness I have placed on them. I release them in the name of Jesus. Amen.

ASK YOURSELF

- Is there anyone toward whom I am holding unforgiveness?

- Was there ever a time I truly let go of unforgiveness?

- What were the effects? How differently did it make me feel?

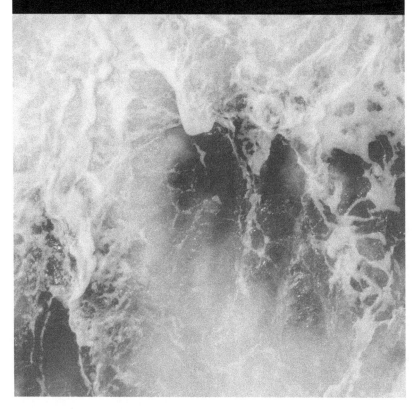

WEEK TWO
FILL ME WITH THE HOLY SPIRIT

DAY EIGHT
SPIRITUAL THIRST

*Jesus answered and said to her, "Whoever drinks of this
water will thirst again, but whoever drinks of the water that
I shall give him will never thirst. But the water that I shall give
him will become in him a fountain of water springing
up into everlasting life."*
John 4:13-14

You did it! You persisted through the painful and difficult
work of emptying yourself of everything that would hinder you
from receiving all God has for you. For the past seven days, you
have humbled yourself, examined yourself, and rid yourself of
the things that only satisfy your flesh. It has not been easy, but it
has been worth it.

For the next seven days, we are setting our hearts toward being filled with the Holy Spirit. The space we have created in our
lives is now about to be filled with the fullness of God. There is
a shift of unprecedented proportions coming into your life. Get
ready for life change.

Chapter four of John's gospel tells us the story of a Samaritan
woman who had a horrible past and present, and her encounter
with Jesus. Jesus went to Samaria and sat next to a well, as His
disciples went to town to purchase some supplies. Jesus asks this
woman to draw some water for Him, which sparks a conversation about thirst, both physical and spiritual, and how nothing
but Jesus can satisfy our spiritual thirst. He tells her that He can

provide water that would become a fountain in us, that would cause us to never be spiritually thirsty ever again.

On the last day, that great day of the feast, Jesus stood and cried out, saying, "If anyone thirsts, let him come to Me and drink. He who believes in Me, as the Scripture has said, out of his heart will flow rivers of living water." But this He spoke concerning the Spirit, whom those believing in Him would receive; for the Holy Spirit was not yet given, because Jesus was not yet glorified.
John 7:37-39

The more we put the polluted waters of the world to our lips, the less we will thirst for Jesus. Many of us no longer have a thirst for the things of God. Many of us have lost our passion, our fire, our desire. We used to pray. We used to spend time in the Word of God. Where did our thirst for the things of God go? When our thirst for Jesus has gone away, it is because we have been drinking from a source other than Him.

We have emptied us of us, and it has exposed a longing inside of us to see God move mightily in us and through us again. We have pushed back the cup of the world. Now it is time to quench our thirst at the cup of Jesus. What we have is what we want. Our spiritual thirst has increased.

We have had enough of faking it. We are done going through the motions of church attendance. We are done putting on a mask of satisfaction, while serving from a dry place. We have walked through a spiritual desert, and have searched diligently for water. We are thirsty for the fresh, living water that only the Holy Spirit can supply.

When Jesus talks about rivers of living water flowing out of us, He is talking about the baptism of the Holy Spirit. John 7 tells us that Jesus was speaking of the time when He would be glorified, return to the Father, and release the Holy Spirit to come and baptize us, as He did in Acts 2. Many today struggle with whether the baptism of the Holy Spirit, experienced by the early church, is for us today.

One of the slickest tricks Satan ever designed was denominationalizing the baptism of the Holy Spirit. To some he says, "You can never have it." To others he says, "You had it, but can never receive it again," and still to another he says, "You have a monopoly on it." We need not struggle to believe it, because the scriptures make it so clear. If we have surrendered our lives to Jesus Christ, no matter your denomination, the baptism of the Holy Spirit is for you, and from this, rivers of living water will flow through you.

Many of us who have been baptized in the Holy Spirit may look at others and scoff that they don't have what we have. However, we must ask ourselves the question: *how long has it been since I have been baptized with the Holy Spirit? How long has it been since I have thirsted for the things of God more than the things of this world?* I want to be so thirsty for God that the world thinks I'm a maniac.

Today we are going to pray that our spiritual thirst not only comes back, but that it would increase day after day, until we long for the things of God like never before.

Let's pray together . . .

Father, in Jesus' name, I ask Your Holy Spirit to increase my thirst for more of Jesus Christ. Let this thirst be so powerful that nothing else can satisfy, except the manifested presence of God. Let the Holy Spirit pour out living water, in and through my soul. I confess that I am thirsty, and I do not want to drink of the waters of this world anymore. I ask You to pour out the waters of Heaven into my life. I ask this in Jesus' name. Amen.

ASK YOURSELF

- Am I thirsting for the things of Heaven or the things of this earth?

- How long has it been since I've cried out for more of God?

- How can I thirst for more of God?

- Have I ever been truly filled with the Spirit?

DAY NINE
SPIRITUAL HUNGER

And Jesus said to them, "I am the bread of life.
He who comes to Me shall never hunger,
and he who believes in Me shall never thirst.
But I said to you that you have seen Me and yet do not believe.
All that the Father gives Me will come to Me,
and the one who comes to Me I will by no means cast out.
For I have come down from heaven, not to do My own will,
but the will of Him who sent Me.
This is the will of the Father who sent Me,
that of all He has given Me I should lose nothing,
but should raise it up at the last day.
And this is the will of Him who sent Me,
that everyone who sees the Son and believes in
Him may have everlasting life; and I will raise him up
at the last day."

The Jews then complained about Him, because He said,
"I am the bread which came down from heaven."
And they said, "Is not this Jesus, the son of Joseph,
whose father and mother we know? How is it then that
He says, 'I have come down from heaven'?"

Jesus therefore answered and said to them,
"Do not murmur among yourselves. No one can come to
Me unless the Father who sent Me draws him;
and I will raise him up at the last day. It is written in the
prophets, 'And they shall all be taught by God.'

*Therefore everyone who has heard and learned from
the Father comes to Me. Not that anyone has seen
the Father, except He who is from God; He has seen the Father.
Most assuredly, I say to you, he who believes in Me has
everlasting life. I am the bread of life. Your fathers ate the
manna in the wilderness, and are dead.
This is the bread which comes down from heaven,
that one may eat of it and not die.
I am the living bread which came down from heaven.
If anyone eats of this bread, he will live forever;
and the bread that I shall give is My flesh,
which I shall give for the life of the world."*

*The Jews therefore quarreled among themselves, saying, "How
can this Man give us His flesh to eat?"*

*Then Jesus said to them, "Most assuredly, I say to you,
unless you eat the flesh of the Son of Man and drink His blood,
you have no life in you. Whoever eats My flesh and drinks
My blood has eternal life, and I will raise him up at the last day.
For My flesh is food indeed, and My blood is
drink indeed. He who eats My flesh and drinks My blood
abides in Me, and I in him. As the living Father sent Me,
and I live because of the Father, so he who feeds on Me
will live because of Me. This is the bread which came down from
heaven—not as your fathers ate the manna, and are dead.
He who eats this bread will live forever."*

*"What then if you should see the Son of Man ascend where He
was before? It is the Spirit who gives life; the flesh profits nothing.
The words that I speak to you are spirit, and they are life."*
John 6:35-58; 62-63

"Ho! Everyone who thirsts,
Come to the waters;
And you who have no money,
Come, buy and eat.
Yes, come, buy wine and milk
Without money and without price.
Why do you spend money for what is not bread,
And your wages for what does not satisfy?
Listen carefully to Me, and eat what is good,
And let your soul delight itself in abundance.
Isaiah 55:1-2

You can always tell when an appetite changes, because it will always produce something different. If our appetites change from the things of God to the things of the world, that hunger will produce the things of the world. Inversely, if our appetites change from the things of the world to the things of God, that hunger will produce the things of God.

What is being produced in your life today? What things are coming from your day-to-day walk, speech, actions, motivations, and passions? If you are primarily producing the things of the world, your appetite has changed from the things of the Spirit to the things of the world. If you are primarily producing the things of the Spirit, your appetite has changed from the things of the world to the things of the Spirit.

If my appetite is for things like reading the Bible, prayer, and worship, both private and corporate, then I have a proper hunger. However, if I don't have an appetite for these things, my hunger is for improper things.

God rained down this food that the people named manna (which means *what?*) every single day. It was unlike anything that anyone had ever seen before or since. Its newness wasn't the only thing that made it unique. No matter how much manna the people of Israel gathered, it would only last for one day. The only exception was the manna they gathered on the day before the Sabbath, which would last through the Sabbath.

Jesus reminds us that the children of Israel ate manna, literally food from heaven, and died. However, whoever consumes Jesus will never die. Why? Because what He is nourishing us with is Spirit and life. Our bodies may go to the grave, but our spirits will live forever with the Lord, because our hunger has been satisfied with the Bread of Life.

None of us would walk into the grocery store or bakery and purchase spoiled, moldy, stale bread to feed ourselves or our families. We wouldn't take it if they offered to give it to us, because not only is it not nourishing, but it can be harmful to us. How many of us are buying and eating the rotten bread of yesterdays, because we do not have fresh bread coming to our lives daily? God is not satisfied with us living off stale and spoiled bread. He does not want us living off yesterday's bread, yesterday's revival, and yesterday's move of God.

When we begin to seek God for a fresh move, a fresh revival, a fresh encounter with the Holy Spirit, we will find that we will be nourished every time we hunger for it. When we find ourselves waking each day with an appetite to see God bring something fresh into our lives, instead of hoarding yesterday's already stale move of God just in case He doesn't come through today, we will find ourselves walking in fresh revelation and power.

The difference between those who walk in the freshness of today's move, and those who continue with the staleness of yesterday's move is appetite. What are we hungry for?

When I am hungry for Jesus, when I have an appetite for communion with the Holy Spirit on a daily basis, when I pull up to the table of prayer, when my desire for His Word is insatiable, when I break the Bread of Life, then my ears, my eyes, and my heart are open to receive the fresh things of Heaven. My discernment, revelation, and prophetic insight are keen to today's needs, challenges, and opportunities.

Sadly, many of us have allowed our spiritual hunger to be replaced with an appetite for worldly bread. This worldly bread will never satisfy our souls. It will never supply what we need. It is an imposter, masquerading as the genuine Bread of Life. This lack of spiritual nourishment has caused us to be spiritually anemic.

We need to get our hunger back for spiritual bread. We need an appetite for the things of God. We need to throw off being satisfied with the mundane. We need to long for the nourishment of the Word, of prayer, and of worship. Our stomachs need to growl in longing for His presence. When we do this, our souls will be satisfied, and our lives will change.

Today, we are going to pray that our hunger for the fresh things of God will increase and that we will no longer live in a state of spiritual malnourishment. Jesus said if we will eat of Him, we will never be hungry again.

Let's pray together . . .

Father, in Jesus' name, I ask Your Holy Spirit to increase my hunger for Jesus, and the things of the Kingdom of God. I confess today that I need fresh bread and that the stale bread of this world will not satisfy. I ask you today to give me fresh bread from Heaven. I repent for allowing my appetite to turn from the things of the Spirit to the things of the world. I ask you to increase my hunger for the Bread of Life. Let me never be satisfied with anything else. Amen.

ASK YOURSELF

- What kind of hunger does my speech, actions, motivations and passions reflect?

- What are some practical ways to align spiritual hunger in my life?

- How can my hunger be satisfied?

- What mundane things do I need to throw off?

DAY TEN
DOING AWAY WITH
WASTEFUL LIVING

For this you know, that no fornicator, unclean person,
nor covetous man, who is an idolater, has any inheritance
in the kingdom of Christ and God. Let no one deceive you
with empty words, for because of these things the wrath of
God comes upon the sons of disobedience.
Therefore do not be partakers with them.

For you were once darkness, but now you are light in the Lord.
Walk as children of light (for the fruit of the Spirit is in
all goodness, righteousness, and truth), finding out what is
acceptable to the Lord. And have no fellowship with the
unfruitful works of darkness, but rather expose them.
For it is shameful even to speak of those things which are
done by them in secret. But all things that are exposed are made
manifest by the light, for whatever makes manifest is light.
Therefore He says:

"Awake, you who sleep, Arise from the dead,
And Christ will give you light."
See then that you walk circumspectly, not as fools but as wise,
redeeming the time, because the days are evil.

Therefore do not be unwise, but understand what the will of the
Lord is. And do not be drunk with wine, in which is dissipation;
but be filled with the Spirit."
Ephesians 5:5-18

The apostle Paul uses two thoughts in this text that show the clear difference of someone who lives to satisfy God, and lives to satisfy themselves. In verse fifteen he says, "see then that you walk circumspectly [carefully], not as fools but as wise." And in verse eighteen he advises us, "do not be drunk with wine, in which is dissipation [or wasteful living]; but be filled with the Spirit."

We are advised to live lives carefully and not wastefully. A wasteful life is a life that is lived to glorify ourselves, our desires, and our agendas with no regard for the purpose of God. A careful life is a life that is lived to glorify God, to be what He desires, to do His will, and to see His purpose fulfilled in our lives.

Imagine with me what our lives would look like if our prayers were prayed differently. Think about what would change if we prayed, "God, what would You have me to do?" instead of "God, I need You to do this for me."

I have been guilty of approaching God with my wants. I have begun a day by laying out a list of demands for the God of Heaven to accomplish on my behalf and closed out with a half-hearted thanks, before I went about the rest of my day. I expect many of us are guilty of this approach.

What if we started our prayers with this question, "God, what do You want from me today?" I can tell you, from personal experience, that the Holy Spirit will answer that prayer.

We are vessels of honor. God wants to move in us and through us. When we humble ourselves and ask God what He desires, instead of demanding what we desire, He will use us as vessels for Himself to be glorified in and through. But to be vessels of honor, we cannot live our lives wastefully. We must be full of the Holy Spirit.

Wasteful living ruins our appetite for Jesus. If someone invited you for supper, having carefully prepared a huge, delicious, nourishing meal, would you stop at the donut shop and scarf down a dozen day-old donuts on the way? Sadly, this is what much of the church is doing today. We are ruining our appetites with wasteful living and are leaving no room for the live-giving filling of the Spirit. Instead of us getting drunk with the wasteful things of this world, we should get drunk on the anointing of the Holy Spirit.

When we are full of the Spirit, our lives become obviously different to anyone who takes notice. When we no longer operate on the limited wisdom of man, and the wasteful conduct of man, it is apparent to all that we are operating in a way that is distinct from everyone else.

Much of the church today operates in a system that thrives in the ways and wisdom of man. Instead of being full of the Holy Spirit, it operates in a system that is easily controlled and predictable. Instead of asking God what he desires for a service, we create agendas that tell Him when and where He can operate, and to what extent He is allowed to move.

As the church of the living God, we must be asking what he wants from our lives, our ministries, our marriages, our work—everything that we do and all that we are. We have to shake off the limited thinking of being satisfied with knowing about the will of God. We can no longer waste our lives merely reading about what God can do. We must earnestly seek Him to find out how He wants to use us for His purpose and His glory. We must desire to hear what He has to say about our lives.

To begin this, we have to ask God to help us stop living wastefully. We need Him to reveal what are God-things and merely good things, because there are things we perceive as good, that are not necessarily sin, but are wasteful, because they do not accomplish the purpose of God in our lives.

We also need to ask Him to baptize us in the Holy Spirit. When we are born again, the Holy Spirit baptizes us into Jesus. However, when we are baptized in the Holy Spirit, Jesus baptizes us in the Spirit. There is a baptism of fire that comes from Jesus and is available to all who are new creations in Christ.

Today, we are going to pray both of these prayers. Pray this with me. . .

Father, in the name of Jesus, I ask You to help me rid my life of wasteful or idle living. I ask You, Lord Jesus, to fill me so full of the Holy Spirit that every thought, every word, and every action flows from You. I surrender this vessel completely to You today. Fill me with Your Spirit. Jesus, I want everything You have for me. Baptize me in the fire of the Spirit, with the evidence of speaking with other tongues. In Jesus' name, I ask this. Amen.

Now, begin to yield to the Holy Spirit and pray in the heavenly language He is giving you.

ASK YOURSELF

- Am I living a purposeful life that glorifies God, or am I wasting time?

- As I seek God, what purpose and plan does He reveal for my life?

- Am I willing to release control and allow God to move?

DAY ELEVEN
INCREASING MY LOVE FOR GOD

*And behold, a certain lawyer stood up and tested Him,
saying, "Teacher, what shall I do to inherit eternal life?"*

*He said to him, "What is written in the law?
What is your reading of it?"*

*So he answered and said, "'You shall love the Lord your God
with all your heart, with all your soul, with all your strength,
and with all your mind,' and 'your neighbor as yourself.'"*

*And He said to him, "You have answered rightly;
do this and you will live."*

*But he, wanting to justify himself, said to Jesus,
"And who is my neighbor?"*

*Then Jesus answered and said: "A certain man went down
from Jerusalem to Jericho, and fell among thieves,
who stripped him of his clothing, wounded him, and departed,
leaving him half dead. Now by chance a certain priest came
down that road. And when he saw him, he passed by
on the other side. Likewise a Levite, when he arrived at the place,
came and looked, and passed by on the other side.
But a certain Samaritan, as he journeyed, came where he was.
And when he saw him, he had compassion.
So he went to him and bandaged his wounds,
pouring on oil and wine; and he set him on his own animal,*

brought him to an inn, and took care of him.
On the next day, when he departed, he took out two denarii,
gave them to the innkeeper, and said to him, 'Take care of him;
and whatever more you spend, when I come again, I will repay
you.' So which of these three do you think was neighbor to him
who fell among the thieves?"

And he said, "He who showed mercy on him."

Then Jesus said to him, "Go and do likewise."
Luke 10:25-37

Here we are at Day Eleven, and what an incredible time this has been. It has not been easy. However, we have persisted because we know the ultimate goal is spiritual restoration and heavenly fire! We have made it to just over the halfway point, and have gone through the painful process of emptying ourselves of our fleshly and worldly works and desires. On Day Eight, as we began to ask God to fill us with more of Him, we prayed to increase our spiritual thirst. Then, we asked Him to increase our spiritual hunger. We asked that He would help us to stop living wastefully. Today, we are asking Him to increase our love for Him.

You might be thinking that spiritual hunger and thirst, and the elimination of wasteful living make sense as we pursue fullness of the Spirit, but that increasing our love for God seems like a waste of our time. We are, however, in the middle of three weeks of fasting and prayer. Shouldn't that be enough proof that we love God? Increasing our love for God increases our capacity to receive a greater fullness of the Holy Spirit. When we walk in the Spirit, we walk in love.

In our scripture reading today, Jesus is tackling two issues. He not only hangs every commandment and prophecy on two things, *You shall love the Lord your God with all your heart, with all your soul, with all your strength, and with all your mind; and your neighbor as yourself,* but he also ties love for God and love for people together. Jesus points out to the questioner what the Bible has pointed out to us all along: the more we love God, the more we will love people. The more we show mercy for people, the more we demonstrate how much we love God. We can never be full of the Holy Spirit and fail to walk in love.

Do not love the world or the things in the world.
If anyone loves the world, the love of the Father is not in him.
For all that is in the world—the lust of the flesh,
the lust of the eyes, and the pride of life—is not of the Father
but is of the world. And the world is passing away,
and the lust of it; but he who does the will of God abides forever.
1 John 2:15-17

If the love of the Father is not in us, we have a good indication that we actually love the world system and the things in the world system. The love of the Father and the love of the world cannot coexist. This we know, but as we push forward to 1 John 3, we see the link.

We know that we have passed from death to life,
because we love the brethren. He who does not love his brother
abides in death. Whoever hates his brother is a murderer,
and you know that no murderer has eternal life
abiding in him. By this we know love,
because He laid down His life for us.

And we also ought to lay down our lives for the brethren.
1 John 3:14-16

If we hate people because of their race, their ethnicity, what they've done to us, or what they've said about us, the Bible tells us that we are a murderer. We know that murderers have no place in the Kingdom of God. If we are to walk in the Spirit, we must walk in love. Remember, all of the commandments hang on love.

He who has My commandments and keeps them,
it is he who loves Me. And he who loves Me will be loved
by My Father, and I will love him and manifest Myself to him.
John 14:21

True Biblical love is not merely spoken; it is proven. We prove this love in what we do. We can say that we love God, but if we do not keep His commandments, we do not love. Our love for God and others has to be proven through our actions. We can make the words *I love you* come from our lips and hate the person we spoke them to in our hearts. For this reason, we have to ask God to increase our love for Him and for people. This is the way to grow in the Spirit, because the Spirit is attracted to love.

As we pray today, I want you to think about your love for God. Is it a love that brings you to obedience? If not, you do not have true Biblical love. Why? Because true love brings us to obedience. It demands it. When we truly love God, we are going to truly love people.

Let's pray together . . .

Father, in the name of Jesus, I ask Your Holy Spirit to help me and to increase my love for you. Holy Spirit, fill me with Your deep love, so I can love Jesus at a deeper level. I confess that I want to be in love with Jesus Christ, and with my neighbor.

Forgive me for walking according to the flesh, and not in love. Forgive me for basing the way I love and treat others on the way they treat me. Forgive me for living for myself.

Teach me to love Jesus. And as I fall more in love with Him, let me love people in the same way. I desire to walk in compassion, just as Jesus walked. May the world know that I am Your disciple because I love others.

I ask this in Jesus' name. Amen.

ASK YOURSELF

- Is my love for God so evident that it is displayed to other people?

- How have I proven, not merely spoken, Biblical love to others?

- Does my love for God lead me to obedience? How do I know?

DAY TWELVE
ABIDING IN THE LOVE OF GOD

*"If you abide in Me, and My words abide in you,
you will ask what you desire, and it shall be done for you.
By this My Father is glorified, that you bear much fruit;
so you will be My disciples.*

*"As the Father loved Me, I also have loved you;
abide in My love. If you keep My commandments,
you will abide in My love, just as I have kept My Father's
commandments and abide in His love.*

*"These things I have spoken to you, that My joy may r
emain in you, and that your joy may be full.
This is My commandment, that you love one another
as I have loved you. Greater love has no one than this,
than to lay down one's life for his friends.
You are My friends if you do whatever I command you.
No longer do I call you servants, for a servant does not know
what his master is doing; but I have called you friends,
for all things that I heard from My Father I have made
known to you. You did not choose Me, but I chose you
and appointed you that you should go and bear fruit,
and that your fruit should remain, that whatever you
ask the Father in My name He may give you.
These things I command you, that you love one another.*

*"If the world hates you, you know that it hated
Me before it hated you. If you were of the world,*

the world would love its own. Yet because you are not of the
world, but I chose you out of the world,
therefore the world hates you."
John 15:7-19

Yesterday, we asked God to increase our love for Him and for others. Today, we are going to learn how to abide in this increased love.

To abide means to live in, or dwell in, in the same way we live in or dwell in our house. It is the place we reside. Abiding in love means that we can be found residing in love. When we are to be found, we can be found in love, if we abide in love. Our reading from the fifteenth chapter of the Gospel of John shows us so many powerful truths about what abiding in love looks like.

As we abide in God, His words abide in us. As this happens, the limits begin to be removed from our lives, and we will have the things we ask for, because they have been requested from a life that is abiding in love. The Father is glorified in this and makes our lives produce fruit. We become walking fruit trees and seed dispensers. Abiding in the love of God and keeping the commands of God cause an increase of joy, even fullness of joy.

Have you ever taken time to think about the way that Jesus loved His disciples? The Bible says that Judas was a snake from the beginning, yet Jesus washed his feet moments before he betrayed Him. Peter would deny Him, Thomas would doubt Him, and they would all run away and leave Him in His darkest time, yet He loved and cared for them all. This is the type of love we must have.

Jesus gives a prerequisite for friendship with Him: obeying His commands. Very often we assume that our church attendance, our one-time prayer at an altar, our water baptism, our Christian to-do list, or our ministry service is what qualifies us for friendship with God. While all these things may play a part, it really comes down to obeying God and doing what He says. It is worth repeating: when we walk in the Spirit, we are walking in love. If we intend to live in the overflow of God, we must abide in love. Abiding in love means I live every day loving God and loving people. It is a lifestyle, not a one-time act.

We love without the need for this love being reciprocated. The world hated Jesus so much that they talked about Him, conspired against Him, falsely accused Him, wrongfully convicted Him, tortured Him, and executed Him. We shouldn't be surprised when we are hated too. We cannot allow this to affect the way we love. Jesus didn't. Being full of the Spirit means we keep a spiritual consciousness that we are not trying to appease the world by being like the world. We make a horrible mistake when we fabricate our lives to be like the world in the hope that we can draw the world to us. The world is not working for darkness; they are looking for light. It is the difference that draws them. We can never be like the world and save the world.

It is love alone that dictates my response to people and to God. John 15 begins with Jesus talking about us abiding in Him as branches abide in a vine. All through the chapter, He shows us what this looks like in how we conduct ourselves. All of this culminates with Him talking about the Holy Spirit.

"But when the Helper comes, whom I shall send to you from the Father, the Spirit of truth who proceeds from the Father,

He will testify of Me."
John 15:26

When we abide in His love, the Holy Spirit comes and accompanies us, and fills us to overflowing. Before we know it, the love of God operates in us and through us in such a way that the things that used to trip us up, keep us awake, hold us back, and make us hate, are no longer able to do any of those things. We become unconquerable when we abide in love.

Today, as we pray, we are going to get honest with the Holy Spirit. He already knows what we have need of, so it's important for us to be honest with Him and ourselves. True confession opens the door for the Helper to do His perfect work.

Let's ask Him to do something special . . .

Father, in the name of Jesus, I ask You to fill me with the love of Jesus in such a way that I am able to love others as much as I love myself. Holy Spirit, I confess to You today that it is hard, at times, for me to love others. It is often difficult for me to show the love of God to people. I ask You to help me with this. Fill me with a love for God, and for people, that I have never had. Let a divine work of the Holy Spirit work in, and through, my heart, mind, and soul. Let every hindrance to my moving forward be removed. Expose every trap of the enemy. Make me wise as a serpent and harmless as a dove. Let every yoke of bondage in my life be destroyed now.

I ask this in Jesus' name. Amen.

ASK YOURSELF

- What does abiding in love look like in my life?

- In what areas of my life do I need to obey the Lord?

- When was the last time I showed the love of God to my family? A coworker? A friend? A stranger?

DAY THIRTEEN
DRAWING NEAR TO GOD

Where do wars and fights come from among you?
Do they not come from your desires for pleasure that war
in your members? You lust and do not have.
You murder and covet and cannot obtain.
You fight and war. Yet you do not have because you do not ask.
You ask and do not receive, because you ask amiss,
that you may spend it on your pleasures.
Adulterers and adulteresses! Do you not know that friendship
with the world is enmity with God?
Whoever therefore wants to be a friend of the world
makes himself an enemy of God. Or do you think that the
Scripture says in vain,
"The Spirit who dwells in us yearns jealously"?

But He gives more grace. Therefore He says:

"God resists the proud,
But gives grace to the humble."
Therefore submit to God. Resist the devil and he will flee
from you. Draw near to God and He will draw near to you.
Cleanse your hands, you sinners; and purify your hearts,
you double-minded. Lament and mourn and weep!
Let your laughter be turned to mourning and your joy to gloom.
Humble yourselves in the sight of the Lord,
and He will lift you up.
James 4:1-10

Before we were born again, we were enemies of God. The Holy Spirit, through the apostle James, uses the word *enmity* to describe the nature of the relationship between the world and God. Enmity means *hostility.* When we were in the world, before Christ Jesus saved us, we were actually hostile toward Him. However, when we accepted Christ, and follow His commands, we became friends, instead of enemies. Now, instead of hostility, the Holy Spirit is now jealous over us. He is an active part of our everyday lives. With the hostility gone, we have this command: *draw near to God.*

Drawing near to God means that we seek after God with our whole heart. This is what prayer and fasting is all about. We are not on a hunger strike to force God to do something. We are foolish to presume we can make God do anything. Instead, we are humbling ourselves through prayer and fasting for God to transform us and position us to walk in His perfect will. We remove the impediments that block our prayers from reaching the ears of God. It is about seeking God with everything in us.

Now the Spirit of God came upon Azariah the son of Oded.
And he went out to meet Asa, and said to him:
"Hear me, Asa, and all Judah and Benjamin.
The Lord is with you while you are with Him.
If you seek Him, He will be found by you;
but if you forsake Him, He will forsake you.
2 Chronicles 15:1-2

God will meet us at our best. When we are putting our best forward, in any area, God meets us there. When we hold onto the things of the world, we are not pursuing God with our best. We cannot expect to have the fullness of God and keep our attachments to the world. I used to say that God will meet us halfway. Sometimes though, the best we can do is to take one step. Whatever we can do, we must do it all, in order to draw nearer to God. With all you have, go after God.

Since you have purified your souls in obeying the truth
through the Spirit in sincere love of the brethren,
love one another fervently with a pure heart.
1 Peter 1:22

When our hearts are polluted, we develop a hardness for the things of God. When our hearts become hardened to the things of God, we cannot draw near to God. To draw near to God, I must purify myself (empty me of me), obey truth through the power of the Holy Spirit, and fervently and sincerely love with a pure heart.

I want you to pray this with me today. . .

Father, in Jesus' name, I ask Your Spirit to quicken me to draw closer to You today. Spirit of God, remind me to pray, to praise, and to be persistent in drawing near to You. Take this discipline from being something I do to being who I am. Father, keep my heart pure. Keep my heart soft. Keep my heart humble in my own eyes.

I ask this is the strong name of Jesus. Amen.

I sense in the Spirit that a holy hush has come into your life as you have prayed this prayer. This is the nearness, the manifested presence of God. Take time to dwell in this now. God will use this time to create a nearness that you have never experienced.

ASK YOURSELF

- What attachments to the world do I need to let go of?

- Is there hard-heartedness or something else hindering me from drawing near to God?

- As I dwell in the closeness of God through prayer, praise, worship, what is He speaking/revealing to me?

- In what way do I feel myself drawing nearer to God?

DAY FOURTEEN
EXPERIENCING THE MANIFESTED PRESENCE OF GOD

*"He who has My commandments and keeps them,
it is he who loves Me. And he who loves Me will be loved
by My Father, and I will love him and manifest Myself to him."*
John 14:21

We see three distinct aspects of God in scripture. God is omniscient, meaning He is all-knowing. He is omnipotent, which means He is all-powerful. He is omnipresent, which means His presence is everywhere.

As we study the manifested presence of God today, it is important to note that though His presence is everywhere, His manifested presence is not. In our passage of scripture today, we see the distinction that Jesus draws between the omnipresence and the manifested presence. Though God is already everywhere, He manifests Himself to those who keep His commandments. In Psalm 16:11, David draws the distinction between the omnipresence and the manifested presence of God with this statement, "In Your presence is fullness of joy; At Your right hand are pleasures forevermore."

Early in my walk with Christ, I fell in love with the manifested presence of God. It has marked me, and it marks our ministry. One of the things I frequently hear from people who come to our church is that they could sense the presence of God from the moment they pulled onto the property. Many have been unable to explain why they would come to this church and just begin to weep as they came through the doors. It's simple: they encountered the manifested presence of God. The manifested presence of God changes us.

> *Then the Lord said to Moses, "Depart and go up*
> *from here, you and the people whom you have*
> *brought out of the land of Egypt, to the land of which*
> *I swore to Abraham, Isaac, and Jacob, saying,*
> *'To your descendants I will give it.'*
> *And I will send My Angel before you, and I will drive*
> *out the Canaanite and the Amorite and the Hittite*
> *and the Perizzite and the Hivite and the Jebusite.*
> *Go up to a land flowing with milk and honey;*
> *for I will not go up in your midst, lest I consume you*
> *on the way, for you are a stiff-necked people."*
> *Exodus 33:1-3*

God tells Moses that they can go and possess the incredible and rich land He promised to them, because He was going to keep the promises He made to their ancestors. He even promised to send an angel with them to help drive out the inhabitants of the land, but He was not going to be with them in manifested presence. He could not stay with them in their disobedience and rebellion, because He would have to destroy them, because of their wickedness.

Something, however, had happened to Moses. He had originally set out with the people of Israel looking for a promise. Now God was offering this promise, but at the expense of His manifested presence. Moses was unwilling to take the promise of God without the presence of God.

Then Moses said to the Lord, "See, You say to me,
'Bring up this people.' But You have not let me know
whom You will send with me. Yet You have said,
'I know you by name, and you have also found grace in My sight.'
Now therefore, I pray, if I have found grace in Your sight,
show me now Your way, that I may know You and that
I may find grace in Your sight. And consider that this
nation is Your people."

And He said, "My Presence will go with you,
and I will give you rest."

Then he said to Him, "If Your Presence does not go with us,
do not bring us up from here. For how then will it be
known that Your people and I have found grace in Your sight,
except You go with us? So we shall be separate,
Your people and I, from all the people who are upon
the face of the earth."
Exodus 33:12-16

Moses told God that the distinction of His people and every-one else, the thing that sets us apart, is the manifested presence of God. No one can know it merely by the promises we walk in or the way we act. What should separate us from the world is the manifested presence of God working in and through our lives. We cannot walk in disobedience and rebellion, but it should go much deeper than that.

When we are assembled together in our church services, we shouldn't be in some dry atmosphere. We shouldn't be looking at our watches after twenty minutes, looking forward to the time we get to hurry out. When we are in the manifested presence of

God, time doesn't even matter. It's a time of refreshing and empowerment, not some dull thing manufactured by people. It is not man's wisdom; it is the breath of God reaching to the depths of our souls. In it, people are healed, delivered, made free, baptized in the Holy Spirit, and made new. Moses had become addicted to the presence of God by spending time with Him at the Tent of Meeting. This is what allowed him to value the presence of God over the promise of God.

Many of us want God to give us fat bank accounts, new houses, new cars, and God can give this to us. However, we tend to want these things without ever pursuing His presence. We should be longing for His manifested presence every day.

When we want the presence of God more than anything, He will show up in all the places we seek Him. There are times I am reading the Word of God, and the manifested presence of God comes in so powerfully that I am unable to read any further, because I am weeping so strongly. This often happens during my times of prayer and times of worship, both private and corporate.

We have been called to the practice of the presence of God. This has become a lost discipline in the church today. Many do not even know how to practice the manifested presence of God, because they have no idea what it even is. In our corporate worship settings, we have become so controlled by getting in and out in a certain amount of time that we leave no space for God to manifest His presence among us. God does not come on our terms.

We desperately need the manifested presence of God. If all we have are promises, we have missed the most important thing. We should not be satisfied to live a day without the manifested presence of God. We should not be satisfied with a church service, a prayer meeting, or any other ministry without the manifested presence of God. It is His presence that will make the difference. Jesus said if we love Him and keep His commandments, He will manifest Himself to us. We were created for this.

As we pray today, let us cry out for the manifested presence of God to become real in our lives.

Father, in Jesus' name, I ask that the presence of God would be manifested in and through my life today. I ask right now for your presence. I need it. I want it. I am no longer willing to live, worship, minster, or work without Your manifested presence in my life. I ask you to grant it to me now. Holy Spirit, let there be regular moments throughout my days that Your presence becomes so real in me, and comes upon me so powerfully, that I begin to weep before You.

I ask this in the name of Jesus. Amen.

ASK YOURSELF

- Can I truly say that I have encountered the manifested presence of God?

- If so, in what ways have my encounters with the manifested presence of God changed me?

- When was the last time I set aside things in my life to pursue His presence?

- Have my motivations been for earthly possessions, promotions, positions, provision or His presence?

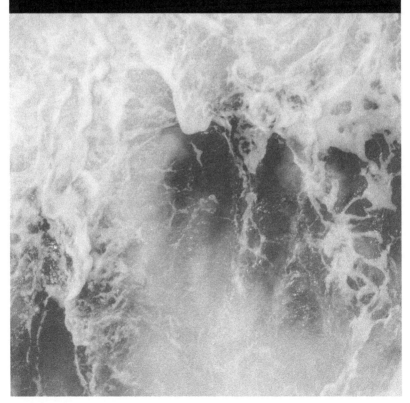

WEEK THREE
OVERFLOWING

DAY FIFTEEN
COMMUNION WITH THE HOLY SPIRIT

The grace of the Lord Jesus Christ, and the love of God,
and the communion of the Holy Spirit be with you all. Amen.
2 Corinthians 13:14

We have made it through fourteen days of prayer and fasting. We have spent a week emptying us of us. We spent a week becoming full of the Holy Spirit. Now, we transition from dealing with what is going on in us to walking in the depth of overflow. I am trusting by faith that you are already beginning to experience the incredible overflow from God.

In order for us to walk in overflow, we have to pass the point where the Holy Spirit moving in our lives is an event, and instead becomes a lifestyle. When we come to a place where the Spirit is inspiring everything we do, say, think, and feel, we are walking in communion, or fellowship, with the Holy Spirit.

When we read both 1 and 2 Corinthians, we see that the apostle Paul, under the inspiration of the Holy Spirit, is correcting many things in the church at Corinth. It is interesting, though, that the last thing he writes to them is to be in communion with the Holy Spirit. He did that because communion with the Holy Spirit will keep us out of, and away from, things designed to entrap us and trip us up. God has an overflow for the body of Christ like we have never seen before, but it will require communion with the Holy Spirit.

Fellowship with the Holy Spirit is a revelation that hit me about six months after I was saved and baptized with the Holy Spirit. I realized that the Holy Spirit was there to guide me on a daily basis. It changed everything about me. I no longer prayed the same, read the Word the same, or ministered the same. I perceived things differently. I understood that being full of the Spirit was not just momentary, but that I was now a carrier of the presence of God.

Now when they had gone through Phrygia and the region
of Galatia, they were forbidden by the Holy Spirit
to preach the word in Asia. After they had come to Mysia,
they tried to go into Bithynia, but the Spirit did not permit them.
So passing by Mysia, they came down to Troas.
And a vision appeared to Paul in the night.
A man of Macedonia stood and pleaded with him,
saying, "Come over to Macedonia and help us."
Now after he had seen the vision, immediately we sought
to go to Macedonia, concluding that the Lord had called us to
preach the gospel to them.
Acts 16:6-10

This passage helps us understand what communing with the Spirit can do for a person. Paul and his team are attempting to go and preach the gospel in several places, but find themselves prevented, not by the forces of darkness, but by the Holy Spirit. We would think that the Spirit would always permit us to preach the gospel everywhere, but He clearly stops Paul. Instead, He gives Paul a vision for the gospel to be preached in Macedonia, and for the first time ever, the message of Jesus Christ goes west, instead of east. This is very good news for we who are westerners.

This came because Paul has such fellowship with the Spirit that he could hear Him say *no* and *yes*.

What if we woke every morning and our number one objective was to commune with the Holy Spirit? What would be different about our lives if we began our days asking Him what He would have us to do with the day He has given us? The direction of the Holy Spirit would take us to places we never dreamed we could go and would allow us to accomplish things we never thought we could accomplish. The Holy Spirit desires to be in fellowship, in communion, in conversation, in revelation with us every single day. He desires to show us things in the Word, in visions, and in dreams.

Today as we pray, we are going to ask God for a deep and continuous communion with the Holy Spirit. We are going to let the Holy Spirit know that we desire this fellowship with Him and that we desire to know what He rejoices in and what grieves Him. This way we will know what pleases Him and what does not please Him. These boundaries are extremely important in relationship. We will ask Him to help us to guard this communion with all we have. From this day on, we will never have to live a day without it.

Father, in the name of Jesus, I ask today for a deep and continuous fellowship with the Holy Spirit. I do not want to be led by my own wisdom any longer. Holy Spirit, let me know what you desire for my life. Let me know what grieves You, and let me know what makes You happy. Quicken me to do exactly that. I desire a deep fellowship with You. Help me guard this every day. I ask these things in Jesus' name. Amen.

ASK YOURSELF

- In what ways has today's devotion change the way I view and respond to the Holy Spirit?

- What boundaries do I need to set up in my life to keep from hurting the feelings of the Holy Spirit?

- What are some things I can do daily to keep me focused on Holy Spirit communion?

DAY SIXTEEN
THE ANOINTING OF THE HOLY SPIRIT

But the anointing which you have received from Him
abides in you, and you do not need that anyone teach you;
but as the same anointing teaches you concerning all things,
and is true, and is not a lie, and just as it has taught you,
you will abide in Him.
1 John 2:27

For the past two days, we have shifted from the two previous weeks. We began by emptying ourselves of the things that were polluting our lives and our walk with God. Then, we filled those emptying places with the Person and Presence of the Holy Spirit. Now, we are learning to walk in a lifestyle that is always abounding, overflowing, in the Holy Spirit. This started with discovering, or rediscovering, that the Holy Spirit really wants to fellowship with us on a constant basis. Today, we are going to go deeper.

The overarching purpose of 1 John is to combat false teaching and false prophecy in the church. The apostle John was clearing up lies that had been perpetrated by people attempting to spread their false beliefs. He is constantly reminding us of the truth we know, and instructs us to abide in this always.

In the Ezekiel 47, God takes the prophet to the temple. As he exits the temple, he steps out into water. The water is at Ezekiel's ankles, and steadily rises the further he walks into it, until it ultimately becomes so deep that the prophet can only swim in it. This water flows out into the sea and heals the stagnant, polluted waters, causing them to be life-producing again. Though this is an end-time prophecy, it has implications for the lives of believers in every age.

Very often in the Old Testament, water represents the presence and work of the Holy Spirit. As we apply the symbolism of this prophecy to our own lives, we can see that there are varying degrees of the anointing of the Holy Spirit we can choose to operate in. For some of us, we operate in an anointing that is only ankle-deep. Some of us are waist-deep, others neck-deep. However, there are mighty currents in the river of God that put us in a position where we no longer have to stand on our own; instead, we can move in the flow of God. This river is taking us where the Holy Spirit wants us to go. We don't tell ourselves where we want to go. That is the right of the Holy Spirit alone. Often, we don't even have an idea of the destination, nor how fast we will arrive there.

God is looking for a people who are not afraid to jump into the flow. He desires a remnant who will allow the flow of God to carry them wherever He chooses for them to go, at the speed he desires. This is the way we move in an anointing one can only swim in. As we do this, God will be able to use us in such mighty ways, our minds won't be able to fathom.

Throughout the Torah (Genesis through Deuteronomy), we see the prevalence of oil. God instructs Moses to create a holy oil for the purposes of anointing. This oil had no power, in and of itself, but what it represented was incredibly powerful. This was used to anoint and empower priests and kings to operate in their respective offices, rule the people, execute justice, and do the will of God for the people of God.

Fast-forward to the Garden of Gethsemane, where Jesus frequently went to pray. Before He went to the cross, He was found there praying. I have been to the Garden of Gethsemane and have seen its ancient trees. Most prevalent are the olive trees. People went to this place to pick olives. These olives were primarily used to make oil. The name *Gethsemane* literally means *oil press*. This was the place they would crush the olives to extract the oil. Without crushing the olives, there could be no flow of oil.

In order to operate in the flow of the anointing, we must understand we have to be crushed. There are times we must face hardship. There are times we must be broken. Because of the situations and circumstances we face on a daily basis, it can often seem like God is not even for us. Life can press on us so hard that it feels like we have been abandoned. Do you know what's happening in these times? We are being broken so the anointing can flow. When we allow these seasons of brokenness, it is creating places where the anointing can flow through us. Oswald Chambers said, "Before God can use a man greatly, He must wound him deeply." This is what was happening with Jesus in the Garden of Gethsemane. He laid His will before God and allowed it to be crushed, until he declared, "not my will, but Yours be done."

If we ever intend to me used powerfully for God, we must visit the oil press often. I must admit that I do not like my times there, until they are over. After they are complete, there is an anointing that is moving in, upon, and through me in a greater way than it ever was before. When it began, I may have only been operating at waist-depth, but when it is finished, I find myself swimming in the flow of God.

It shall come to pass in that day
That his burden will be taken away from your shoulder,
And his yoke from your neck,
And the yoke will be destroyed because of the anointing oil.
Isaiah 10:27

If we are going to see the bondage destroyed in our lives and the lives of the people around us, we are going to have to visit the oil press, again and again. If we don't, the anointing cannot flow, and at best we are giving them only what we can provide. We owe ourselves and the people around us the supernatural, bondage-breaking anointing. There are people whom Satan has bound in sickness, addiction, pornography, idolatry, self-righteousness, poverty, and racism. However, when the anointing hits these yokes, they are destroyed, and we can be led by the Holy Spirit. God wants us operating in the full flow of the anointing of the Holy Spirit.

Think about yourself over the past couple of weeks. How many breakthroughs have you experienced? How many people have you been able to forgive? How many bondages have you been able to shake off? How many times have you become overwhelmed by the power and presence of God? All of these have come at the level you have allowed yourselves to be crushed.

We must confess before God our desire to get out of the ankle-depth and waist-depth we have been operating in. We need to ask God for such an increase that we would only be able to swim in it. We must pray that we may only flow with the River of God.

Let's pray together . . .

Father, in the name of Jesus, I ask for the Holy Spirit to move in my life and help me to have an increased anointing, in and upon my life, my ministry, my family, and my church. I desire, this day, to live in an anointing that I can only swim in. Let a mighty anointing stir up in me right now. I submit to the pressing. Help me to keep a right perception through it. I commit to cherish and protect this anointing. I thank You for the anointing, God, and I ask all of this in Jesus' name. Amen.

ASK YOURSELF

- In what ways do I sense God calling me deeper into His heavenly river?

- How have I been crushed so that my oil could flow?

- In what ways am I willing to be crushed to allow more oil to flow?

DAY SEVENTEEN
FRESH FIRE

When the Day of Pentecost had fully come,
they were all with one accord in one place.
And suddenly there came a sound from heaven,
as of a rushing mighty wind,
and it filled the whole house where they were sitting.
Then there appeared to them divided tongues,
as of fire, and one sat upon each of them.
And they were all filled with the Holy Spirit and began to speak
with other tongues, as the Spirit gave them utterance.
Acts 2:1-4

Let me go ahead and prepare you: this is about to get good. When I first shared this word with our ministry, the power and presence of God was so strong that it became necessary to extend the devotional time, as the fire of God began to fall.

When my wife and I first became born-again, the Lord saved us from a very rough past. We were already married when we accepted Christ. We realized that we didn't know who we really were before, and struggled that first week of being born-again. So, we decided that our marriage was a mistake, and cordially and calmly decided that we would divorce, and live for the Lord separately.

The following Sunday, we came to church, and my pastor preached on the baptism in the Holy Spirit. Though I had heard about the Holy Spirit as a child, I had never been taught about Him the way I was that day. As my pastor preached, a hunger began to build inside of me, and by the time he gave the call to be baptized in the Holy Spirit, with the evidence of speaking with other tongues, I was ready. Though the church was packed, only a few of us responded to the altar call that day. My pastor and another man began to pray for me, and suddenly, deep inside of me, something began to bubble up. All of a sudden, I began to speak with other tongues. This was unlike anything I had ever experienced before. It was like there was a river flowing into me and out of me at the same time. When I left the church that day, I remember that the colors were more vivid and vibrant than I had ever seen them. The God of heaven and earth had made His home inside of me! After this experience, I pulled the idea of divorce off the table. However, we continued to struggle for several more months.

About nine months later, we found ourselves in another service where people were seeking the baptism of the Holy Spirit. Though my wife had not yet been baptized with the Holy Spirit, she went to the altar to pray for her friend, who was seeking it for herself. As my wife laid her hand on her friend, she was gloriously baptized in the Holy Spirit. All these years later, we are still married. Why? There was a power we didn't have that God deposited on the inside of us that gave us what we needed to stay together.

Regardless of denomination, the baptism of the Holy Spirit is available to all believers. Because of my testimony, and what the power of God did in my life, I am passionate about every person who is saved being baptized in the Holy Spirit and fire. You need to be baptized in the Holy Spirit.

It is important to allow scripture to define what we believe. Acts 2 shows us the first time that the church was baptized in the

Holy Spirit. Fifty days after Jesus was raised from the dead, and ten days after He ascended to the Father, we find the disciples among 120 believers in an upper room on the Day of Pentecost. They are all praying into the command and promise that Jesus gave them.

> *And being assembled together with them,*
> *He commanded them not to depart from Jerusalem,*
> *but to wait for the Promise of the Father, "which," He said,*
> *"you have heard from Me; for John truly baptized with water,*
> *but you shall be baptized with the Holy Spirit not many days*
> *from now." Therefore, when they had come together,*
> *they asked Him, saying, "Lord, will You at this time restore*
> *the kingdom to Israel?" And He said to them,*
> *"It is not for you to know times or seasons which the*
> *Father has put in His own authority.*
> *But you shall receive power when the Holy Spirit*
> *has come upon you; and you shall be witnesses to*
> *Me in Jerusalem, and in all Judea and Samaria,*
> *and to the end of the earth."*
> *Acts 1:4-8*

After praying for ten days, these people received the promised baptism of the Holy Spirit. They received this power. When this power came, they began to speak with other tongues as the Spirit enabled them. This is what we all need today!

I know there are differing views on this, but the Bible does not waver on it. We cannot allow someone's teaching, someone's position papers, or someone's book define truth. We must allow the Bible to define truth. If the Bible says it is true, it is truth.

I indeed baptize you with water unto repentance,
but He who is coming after me is mightier than I,
whose sandals I am not worthy to carry.
He will baptize you with the Holy Spirit and fire.
Matthew 3:11

The *He* John the Baptist is referring to here is Jesus. It is Jesus who baptizes us in the Holy Spirit. However, just a few verses later, we see that Jesus Himself was baptized in the Holy Spirit.

When He had been baptized, Jesus came up immediately from
the water; and behold, the heavens were opened to Him,
and He saw the Spirit of God descending like a dove
and alighting upon Him. And suddenly a voice came
from heaven, saying, "This is My beloved Son,
in whom I am well pleased."
Matthew 3:16-17

Then Jesus, being filled with the Holy Spirit, returned from the
Jordan and was led by the Spirit into the wilderness.
Luke 4:1

Jesus did not do one miracle, preach one message, call one disciple, heal one person, cast out one demon, or raise one person from the dead until He had been filled with the Holy Spirit. If Jesus, the Son of the living God, had to be filled with the Holy Spirit, who are we to say that we do not need to be baptized with the Holy Spirit to do the work of the ministry? What the church needs in these last days is an army of people who are baptized in the Holy Spirit.

If we have confessed our sins, repented of our sins, and have confessed the resurrected Jesus as our Lord and Savior, we are blood-bought believers. This is a wonderful work of grace, but is not the same as being baptized in the Holy Spirit. Salvation cleanses us of sin, and secures our eternity with Christ, but it also qualifies and entitles us to be baptized in the Holy Spirit, with the evidence of speaking with other tongues. Salvation and the baptism in the Holy Spirit are not the same thing. When we are born again, the Spirit baptizes us into Jesus.

> *For as the body is one and has many members,*
> *but all the members of that one body, being many,*
> *are one body, so also is Christ. For by one Spirit we were*
> *all baptized into one body—whether Jews or Greeks,*
> *whether slaves or free—and have all been made to drink into*
> *one Spirit. For in fact the body is not one member but many.*
> *1 Corinthians 12:12-14*

It is the work of the Holy Spirit to convict us of sin and draw us to God. He baptizes us into the body of Christ. Then, something remarkable happens; Jesus baptizes us in the Holy Spirit!

> *I indeed baptize you with water unto repentance,*
> *but He who is coming after me is mightier than I,*
> *whose sandals I am not worthy to carry.*
> *He will baptize you with the Holy Spirit and fire.*
> *Matthew 3:11*

Jesus is the Holy Spirit and Fire Baptizer! Now we understand why Jesus told the disciples to go and wait in Jerusalem. They were baptized into Jesus. They were believers. However, now He needed to baptize them in the Holy Spirit. They went to the upper room to be endued with this power from on high, and they received it. The evidence that they received it was that they began to speak with other tongues. Speaking with other tongues was not the baptism of the Holy Spirit, but was the outward evidence of the inward empowerment.

And they were all filled with the Holy Spirit and began to speak
with other tongues, as the Spirit gave them utterance.
Acts 2:4

We see this happen again in Acts 10 as the apostle Peter preached in the house of Cornelius.

While Peter was still speaking these words,
the Holy Spirit fell upon all those who heard the word.
And those of the circumcision who believed were astonished,
as many as came with Peter, because the gift of the Holy Spirit
had been poured out on the Gentiles also.
For they heard them speak with tongues and magnify God.
Acts 10:44-46

Then it happens again.

And it happened, while Apollos was at Corinth, that Paul, hav-
ing passed through the upper regions, came to Ephesus.
And finding some disciples he said to them, "Did you receive the
Holy Spirit when you believed?"

So they said to him, "We have not so much as heard whether
there is a Holy Spirit."

And he said to them, "Into what then were you baptized?"

So they said, "Into John's baptism."

*Then Paul said, "John indeed baptized with a baptism
of repentance, saying to the people that they should believe
on Him who would come after him, that is, on Christ Jesus."*

*When they heard this, they were baptized in the name of the
Lord Jesus. And when Paul had laid hands on them,
the Holy Spirit came upon them, and they spoke
with tongues and prophesied.*
Acts 19:1-6

It is very clear in scripture that we can and should be speaking with other tongues.

*Therefore, brethren, desire earnestly to prophesy,
and do not forbid to speak with tongues.*
1 Corinthians 14:39

Unfortunately, many churches today defy scripture by forbidding people to speak in tongues. We have allowed ourselves to get to a place that we don't want a thing if we cannot figure it out with our natural minds. Therefore, we have created a natural god of humanism, instead of a God who is supernatural, who transforms humans.

Before we move forward, we need to address the one scripture most often used to try to dissuade people from speaking with other tongues.

Love never fails. But whether there are prophecies,
they will fail; whether there are tongues, they will cease;
whether there is knowledge, it will vanish away.
For we know in part and we prophesy in part.
But when that which is perfect has come,
then that which is in part will be done away.

When I was a child, I spoke as a child,
I understood as a child, I thought as a child;
but when I became a man, I put away childish things.
For now we see in a mirror, dimly, but then face to face.
Now I know in part, but then I shall know just
as I also am known.

And now abide faith, hope, love, these three;
but the greatest of these is love.
1 Corinthians 13:8-13

Most often, when someone wants to validate the belief that speaking in tongues is not for the church of today, they use this portion of verse 8: *whether there are tongues, they will cease.* However, it is important to look at the entire context of this passage of scripture to determine when the time is right for the cessation of tongues.

For we know in part and we prophesy in part.
But when that which is perfect has come,
then that which is in part will be done away.

For now we see in a mirror, dimly, but then face to face.
Now I know in part, but then I shall know just
as I also am known.

Have we learned everything there is to know? Have all prophecies been fulfilled? Of course not. All these things are partial, until we meet Jesus. When we see Jesus face-to-face, then everything that is vague and partial will become clear and full. Until that time comes, we have knowledge, prophecy, and tongues.

The baptism in the Holy Spirit is for you right now. He wants you filled with His fire. He wants you empowered by His presence working in you and through you; and yes, He wants you to speak with other tongues. I know this may seem outrageous, but let's consider what we who are born-again already believe.

- We believe that God the Father sent His only Son to the earth, and that He was born to a virgin.
- We believe this virgin-born man-God lived an entirely sinless life.
- We believe that He performed many miracles such as turning water into wine, healing blind people, walking on water, multiplying food, and raising dead people to life.
- We believe that He was executed on a cross, for doing no wrong.
- We believe that He was placed into a grave, where He remained for three days.
- We believe He was resurrected from the dead.
- We believe that He walked on the earth for forty days, and many people witnessed this.
- We believe that He ascended into heaven in plain sight of many people.
- We believe that He is returning to rapture His church one day.

Is it so far-fetched to believe that He can give us a heavenly language?

The same faith it took for you to be born again is the same faith it will take to be filled with the Holy Spirit. I believe that this faith has been strengthened today, and that as we pray, Jesus is about to baptize you in the Holy Spirit and with fire!

We will pray together today, and when that is finished, I am going to pray over you. As I do this, there will be some syllables, unknown to you, that you will begin to hear in your inner self. When you hear them, I want you to begin to speak them aloud. In the same way that it happened to me, rivers of living water with flow in you and out of you, at the same time. This is the baptism of the Holy Spirit and fire.

Let's pray together . . .

Father, in the name of Jesus, I humble myself this day, and I ask You to forgive me of any and all sin. I repent of it, and turn from it. I believe and receive, by faith, Jesus Christ as Lord and Savior. I thank You for saving me.

Father, I believe Your Word more than anyone else or anything else. Your Word says that my Lord and Savior, Jesus, baptizes with the Holy Spirit and fire.

Jesus, in Your name, I ask for all You have for me. I desire it. Baptize me with the Holy Spirit and fire, with the evidence of speaking in other tongues. By faith, I receive it, in Your name.

Now yield to the Spirit as I pray this over you . . .

Father, I sense in my spirit that Your people are hungry and thirsty for You. They believe there is so much more than what they have. Jesus, You said this is Your promise. So I ask now that there would be a powerful baptism of the Holy Spirit and fire that would fall now. Jesus, I ask that you would gloriously baptize them in the Holy Spirit and with fire. Give them their prayer language right now. As they begin to speak it, let the rivers of living water flow in them and out of them.

I declare over you, in the name of Jesus, be baptized in the Holy Spirit and fire, right now!

ASK YOURSELF

- When was the last time I experienced God's fresh fire in my life?

- In what ways did His fire change me? How did it change my perspective on life, my feelings toward others and my relationship with God?

- Is there room in my life for more fresh fire? Do I want more today?

DAY EIGHTEEN
DREAMS AND VISIONS

And it shall come to pass afterward
That I will pour out My Spirit on all flesh;
Your sons and your daughters shall prophesy,
Your old men shall dream dreams,
Your young men shall see visions.
And also on My menservants and on My maidservants
I will pour out My Spirit in those days.
Joel 2:28-29

Let's talk about some of the ways the Lord speaks to us.

First and foremost, He speaks through His Word, the Bible. Any time He speaks by any other means, it will always line up with His Word.

He speaks to us in prayer.

He speaks to us through other believers, our leaders, and prophets.

He speaks through visions and dreams.

As we have gone through this process, first emptying ourselves of us, then being filled with the Holy Spirit, and now overflowing with the power and presence of God, we are positioned for God to speak to us in unprecedented ways. I believe that God is about to open the heavens and speak to you in visions and dreams, like never before.

There are several places in scripture that God used this means to communicate to His people. Often, these were nation-shifting. Always they were life-changing. Sometimes they were life-saving. In one case, it even protected the life of Jesus, the Messiah. Here are some examples of God speaking to people through dreams and visions: Genesis 37; Genesis 41; Matthew 2; and Acts 10.

When we have a dream or see a vision, the first thing we must do is ask God, "Is this from You?" When we have determined through His Word and His manifested presence that it is from Him, we must next ask, "What do I do with this?" He gave it to us for a reason, so we must find out the reason.

We live a supernatural life with God, so we must not think it strange that God will give us supernatural visions and dreams. We may not have them often, but when we live in the overflow, we can expect them at any time.

You can be spiritual and have visions and dreams without being crazy. God is real enough. He does not need our help making Him more real. Many people are turned off to the supernatural because people do not know how to respond properly to the revelation they receive from God. We don't have to tell just anyone about what we are shown. When God gives us a vision and tells us to communicate it to someone, we can do it humbly and with a spirit of love. We cannot allow our flesh to overtake us in our response. We don't have to turn cartwheels in the sanctuary or shout from the rooftops to prove we have received a word from God. The supernatural is enough to draw people to God. We don't need to make it extra-supernatural. Take this as a word of caution: do not allow yourself to operate in the flesh and add to the dream or vision given to us by God. Stay in the Spirit, and obey God.

Not everyone will receive this from you. Do not allow rejection to shut it down in your life. We are living in the last days, and God has promised that He would speak to us in dreams and visions in the last days. We should expect Him to speak to us in this way. Today, we are going to pray that God will increase our capacity to receive from Him in dreams and visions. We are going to ask Him to release visions, dreams, and prophetic words into our lives, for such a time as this. We will commit our bodies as vessels of honor to God, so He can use us to speak in these last days.

Let's pray . . .

Father, in Jesus' name, I ask you today to pour out Your Spirit upon me in such a way that it would release dreams, visions, and prophetic words into my life, for such a time as this. I commit my body as a vessel to You, and I am willing to be used by You, in these last days, in whatever way you want to use me. Quicken me with prayer to seek the interpretations of the visions, dreams, and prophetic words You give to me. Keep me from operating in the flesh. Let me always operate in the Spirit. I ask this in the name of Jesus. Amen.

ASK YOURSELF

- When God speaks, how will I respond?

- How has God spoken directly to me in the past?

- Will I allow God to reveal things to me that will forever change me?

DAY NINETEEN
SEEING WHAT GOD SEES

That the God of our Lord Jesus Christ, the Father of glory,
may give to you the spirit of wisdom and revelation in the
knowledge of Him, the eyes of your understanding being
enlightened; that you may know what is the hope
of His calling, what are the riches of the glory of His inheritance
in the saints, and what is the exceeding greatness
of His power toward us who believe, according to the working
of His mighty power which He worked in Christ when
He raised Him from the dead and seated Him at
His right hand in the heavenly places, far above
all principality and power and might and dominion,
and every name that is named,
not only in this age but also in that which is to come.
Ephesians 1:17-21

You are in a season of overflow!

Think about how far you've come so quickly. I know these nineteen days have seemed long, until you really put it in perspective. Only two weeks ago, you were emptying yourself of the things in your life that were preventing the fullness of God operating in and through you. Since then you have opened doors to being full of the Holy Spirit, even hearing God speak through visions and dreams!

When I read Ephesians 1:17-21, it is difficult to not personalize it. I pray this prayer over myself very often. I pray this prayer so often because I realize that God wants me to see in the spirit realm.

The spirit realm is more real than the natural realm we live, work, and function in every day. Sadly, many of us do not acknowledge it or even know it exists because we lack the ability to see it. We need our understanding to be opened to be able to comprehend the spirit realm.

It is doubtless not profitable for me to boast.
I will come to visions and revelations of the Lord:
I know a man in Christ who fourteen years ago—
whether in the body I do not know, or whether out
of the body I do not know, God knows—such a one was caught
up to the third heaven. And I know such a man—
whether in the body or out of the body I do not know,
God knows—how he was caught up into Paradise and heard
inexpressible words, which it is not lawful for a man to utter.
2 Corinthians 12:1-4

The Bible tells us there are three heavens. We can also call them three dimensions or realms. The first is the one we live in, right here on earth. The third realm is the place where God's throne is. There is no evil, sin, sickness, death, loss, or sadness in this realm.

The second is the heaven between where we are and the throne of God. This is the realm where the spiritual battle is going on. This is the realm we need the greatest insight into.

For we do not wrestle against flesh and blood, but against
principalities, against powers, against the rulers
of the darkness of this age, against spiritual hosts
of wickedness in the heavenly places.
Ephesians 6:12

Often, we assume nothing is happening if we cannot see it, but this is not the case at all. Think about it like this. If there was work occurring outside of the place you are in, and you could not see it, would it mean that the work would not actually be happening, because of your inability to see it? Or if you cannot see inside the grocery store across town, would that mean that no one is shopping? Absolutely not. However, this is how many of us choose to live our lives. We are saved, filled with the Spirit, and faithful to God and His church, but we are oblivious to the fact that Satan is constantly working in this realm, and so is the heavenly host.

Now that we have an understanding of the different dimensions that simultaneously exist, we can ask that the eyes of our understanding be enlightened to see into the spirit realm, where the war is occurring. We can ask that God will show us what is happening, so we will not be ignorant of the tactics of our enemy. We need God to enlighten the eyes of our understanding, so we can see what He sees.

We need this because it will not only expose that there is a spirit realm, but it will also allow us to see what is happening in this realm, allowing us to understand how we must do battle. It is not enough to have wisdom and knowledge; we must also have understanding.

Get wisdom! Get understanding!
Do not forget, nor turn away from the words of my mouth.
Do not forsake her, and she will preserve you;
Love her, and she will keep you.
Wisdom is the principal thing;
Therefore get wisdom.

And in all your getting, get understanding.
Proverbs 4:5-7

The eyes of our understanding must be enlightened, so we may know the hope of His calling. This way we don't have a mere surface understanding or knowledge of what His call is. Instead, we can know the depth of His calling. We can know what He wants to do with our calling.

The eyes of our understanding must be opened, so we may know the riches of the glory of His inheritance in the saints. When we have this, we will never look at our brothers and sisters the same way. We will see the giftings, talents, and treasure that God has placed inside of them. This will also help us, as leaders, parents, and spouses to have a greater realization of our call, which is to help those we've been given to reach their full potential in Christ.

The eyes of our understanding must be opened, so we might know what is the exceeding greatness of His power toward us who believe, according to the working of His mighty power which He worked in Christ when He raised Him from the dead and seated Him at His right hand in the heavenly places.

Every day, I ask that the same power that raised Christ from the dead would dwell in and be at work in me, through me, and upon me, for the glory of His name. This is what He desires for all of us, but if the eyes of our understanding are not enlightened, we won't even know that this power is available to us, nor how to walk in it. We need the scales taken off our eyes. We need Him to show us clearly what is happening, and what we need to do to continue to function in this power. Think about it. If all of us who claim salvation walked in the same power that raised Christ from the dead, it would be very difficult to find a lost person.

Christ is seated far above all principality and power and might and dominion, and every name that is named, not only in this age but also in that which is to come. It is tough to fight a battle that we don't even know exists. It is difficult to have a strategy when we have no idea where the battleground is. We must understand this when our eyes are enlightened to see into the spirit realm, and we see the battle that is happening over and around us, and that Christ is over it all.

So many of us are led by what we see in the natural realm. As believers, we live in the natural, but we are to function, operate, and live in the supernatural. Our faith is supernatural. Healings and miracles are supernatural. The rapture of the church is supernatural. This is the realm we are called to live in. We can work, go to school, go to the ballfield, and go the store in the natural, all while listening and seeing in the supernatural.

In the Book of Acts, we see this on display. These people were making tents, feeding the hungry, and functioning in their daily lives. All the while, they were discerning and living in the supernatural. They were doing everyday life, but allowing the supernatural to break into their natural, and they changed the earth as they knew it.

This overflow you have been experiencing has merely scratched the surface. When the eyes of your understanding are enlightened, you will walk in unprecedented outpouring from God. God is about to open up a realm that is not bound by time, geography, or human capability. God is going to allow you to function in the realm that Jesus functioned in. You will be able to stand in one place, and someone will be healed in another place. You will be in your house, but see the war-planning room of the enemy. This is the realm God has opened for us, and is calling us to. It will require the eyes of our understanding to be enlightened. As this comes, wisdom and revelation will come. God will overflow in us.

Pray this with me . . .

Father, in the name of Jesus, I ask You to enlighten the eyes of my understanding, so I can see what You see. I ask You to give me insight into the spirit realm, so that I may know and understand the battle that is happening over me and around me. Help me, Lord, by giving me a strategy to manifest Your victory. Grant me that the eyes of my understanding be enlightened, that I may know what is the hope of Your calling, what are the riches of the glory of Your inheritance in the saints, and what is the exceeding greatness of Your power toward I who believe, according to the working of Your mighty power which You worked in Christ when You raised Him from the dead and seated Him at Your right hand in the heavenly places, far above all principality and power and might and dominion, and every name that is named, not only in this age but also in that which is to come. Help me. Fill me. Flow through me. Give me power, just like Jesus Christ, to heal the sick, cast out demons, and do good works. Grant it for Your glory, in Jesus' name. Amen.

ASK YOURSELF

- Why is my gaining wisdom, knowledge and understanding so important?

- How can I practice living in the supernatural?

- What scriptures are important for me to pray over my life every day?

DAY TWENTY
FAITH AND ACTION

For I say, through the grace given to me, to everyone
who is among you, not to think of himself more highly
than he ought to think, but to think soberly,
as God has dealt to each one a measure of faith.
Romans 12:3

Overflow is operating with faith in the supernatural. It makes what was impossible become possible. This is what happens when we have faith in God and walk in the supernatural.

I have often encountered people who have told me that they do not have faith. However, the scripture says that God has given to each one a measure of faith. If you are sitting in a chair right now, you are exercising a measure of faith that the chair is going to support you. If you drove today, you exercised a measure of faith in the vehicle you drove. It may be small, or it may be greater, but you have a measure of faith.

What we need to do is take the faith we have and apply it in the supernatural Kingdom of God. This is where God begins to show up in a mighty way.

For in it the righteousness of God is revealed from faith to faith;
as it is written, "The just shall live by faith."
Romans 1:17

If we are going from faith to faith, it means that God is permitting and expecting our faith to grow. Where we were two years ago in our faith is not where we should be today. It should be ever-increasing. Faith is like a muscle. The more we work it, the bigger it gets.

> *But without faith it is impossible to please Him,*
> *for he who comes to God must believe that He is,*
> *and that He is a rewarder of those who diligently seek Him.*
> *Hebrews 11:6*

If we do not have faith, we cannot please God. Our relationship with God is based on faith. When we became born-again, no one could prove our salvation by something they could give us. Even if they gave us a certificate that said we were saved, it means nothing. Our salvation is proven by the faith we have placed in the Lord Jesus Christ to forgive our sins and cleanse us of our unrighteousness. Just as we exercised faith to be born again, we continue to live for God by faith. It takes faith to have a day-to-day relationship with Jesus Christ. It takes faith to pray, witness, give, and minister. Everything about our relationship with God is based on faith. That's why it's impossible to please Him without it.

Almost every time Jesus rebuked His disciples, it was for a lack of faith. This is how God views faith. Lack of it draws rebuke from Him. We have to live by faith, and it must always be growing. This is why the tests and trials come into our lives. This is the purpose for God allowing things to come at us that only He can fix. All this increases our faith. This allows God's supernatural power to manifest in us in greater ways.

Just because we have earthly limitations does not mean we are completely limited. If I can have faith in God's supernatural power, I can override natural limits. My body may be limited to be in one place at one time, but my spirit is not limited in this way. The resources of the Kingdom of God are endless, but they can only be obtained by faith.

Beware, brethren, lest there be in any of you an evil heart of unbelief in departing from the living God; but exhort one another daily, while it is called "Today," lest any of you be hardened through the deceitfulness of sin. For we have become partakers of Christ if we hold the beginning of our confidence steadfast to the end, while it is said:

> *"Today, if you will hear His voice, Do not harden your hearts*
> *as in the rebellion." For who, having heard, rebelled?*
> *Indeed, was it not all who came out of Egypt, led by Moses?*
> *Now with whom was He angry forty years?*
> *Was it not with those who sinned,*
> *whose corpses fell in the wilderness?*
> *And to whom did He swear that they would not enter His rest,*
> *but to those who did not obey?*
> *So we see that they could not enter in because of unbelief.*
> *Hebrews 3:12-19*

God calls unbelief *evil*. We don't want to have an evil heart of unbelief. We don't want to become so wicked that we only believe in what we see with our natural eyes. We are not to be led by what we see, but by what we hear from God. So many of us are bound by the natural realm. We look at our situations, determine what we can do, and fabricate and cultivate an outcome based upon our ability to produce.

However, when we have faith, these bondages cease. We are then vessels of faith that the supernatural can operate through. This was how the prophet Elijah could speak to the widow and tell her that her oil and meal would not run out. This was how the prophet Elisha could tell a widow to borrow as many vessels as she could find and fill those vessels up with the tiny bit of oil she had left in her house. Through faith in God, they were able to tap into the realm of the Spirit, see the unlimited resources, and make it manifest in the natural. In this same way, people are saved, healed, delivered, and provided for. By faith.

Then He spoke a parable to them,
that men always ought to pray and not lose heart,
saying: "There was in a certain city a judge
who did not fear God nor regard man.
Now there was a widow in that city; and she came to him,
saying, 'Get justice for me from my adversary.'
And he would not for a while; but afterward he said
within himself, 'Though I do not fear God
nor regard man, yet because this widow troubles me
I will avenge her, lest by her continual
coming she weary me.' "

Then the Lord said, "Hear what the unjust judge said.
And shall God not avenge His own elect who cry out day and
night to Him, though He bears long with them?
I tell you that He will avenge them speedily.
Nevertheless, when the Son of Man comes,
will He really find faith on the earth?"
Luke 18:1-8

Jesus uses a parable to describe persistence in faith. He uses the example of a widow demanding justice from a person who is unjust in their nature. She continues to believe that she will be avenged, and because of her persistence in this belief, she receives it. He then brings up that God is not unjust and will answer His people. Then he closes with this question, "When the Son of Man comes, will He really find faith on the earth?" God is asking if His people will really have faith.

Many of the attacks you face have very little to do with the thing being attacked. They have very little to do with who you are. They have to do with who you are becoming. Therefore, Satan attacks your *now,* so he can attack your future. It is an assault against your faith, to keep you from your destiny. If we can allow our faith to be stirred and built, we can ward off the attacks and secure our future.

Pray with me . . .

Father, in the name of Jesus, I ask You to help me to put into action the faith that has been given to me. I ask for an increased boldness to use this faith as You see fit. I ask that the measure of faith I have to be increased. Let Your Word continually unlock greater faith in me. Let it rise up in me in a way I have never known before. Let me operate in a supernatural way that is unprecedented in my life. Help me to lean on the arm of the Spirit, and not the arm of the flesh, for cursed is everyone who relies on the arm of the flesh, but blessed are those who lean on the arm of the Spirit. Let me not be led by what I see with my natural eyes, but be led by the Spirit. I thank You for this, in Jesus' name. Amen.

ASK YOURSELF

- How can I practice exercising the "muscle" of faith in a greater way?

- What are ways I can look beyond my own abilities and rely more on God?

- What unlimited resources do I need to tap in to today?

- How can I rise up to counter attacks against my faith?

DAY TWENTY-ONE
THE FULLNESS OF GOD

To know the love of Christ which passes knowledge;
that you may be filled with all the fullness of God.

Now to Him who is able to do exceedingly abundantly above all
that we ask or think, according to the power that works in us.
Ephesians 3:19-20

Here we are . . . Day Twenty-One. You have fasted. You have prayed. You have sought God. Now you are walking in the reward, and it is great!

Now is not the time to quit. You have established a pattern that will continue, if you will continue in it. What we found is that God kept us on a continual cycle of being emptied, and filled again, taking us to greater levels of overflow.

To keep this up, we have two additional devotions to help you continue the process.

As we begin today's devotion, I want you to begin removing every limit in your mind regarding God. I want you to really start to believe that nothing is impossible with Him.

Our scripture reading today tells us that in order to walk in the overflow of God, we must go way beyond what we can fathom. Paul prayed the following over the Ephesians, and this is another prayer I like to pray over myself. This prayer uncovers the process that we must submit to in order to walk in this overflow.

*That He would grant you, according to the riches of His glory,
to be strengthened with might through His Spirit in the inner
man, that Christ may dwell in your hearts through faith;
that you, being rooted and grounded in love,
may be able to comprehend with all the saints what is the width
and length and depth and height—to know the love of Christ
which passes knowledge; that you may be filled with
all the fullness of God.*

*Now to Him who is able to do exceedingly abundantly
above all that we ask or think, according to the power that works
in us, to Him be glory in the church by Christ Jesus to all
generations, forever and ever. Amen.*
Ephesians 3:16-21

First, we must have the strength of Christ inside of us in order to understand the love of Christ. Our human knowledge is so limited. It can only derive from what we have experienced. The love of Christ goes way beyond anything we could have learned and experienced in the natural. The Bible tells us that while we were still sinners, Christ died for us. No natural mind can comprehend this.

Once we know this love, which passes knowledge, we can be filled with the fullness of God. The Bible tells us here that it is possible to be filled with the fullness of God. If it were not possible, the Bible would not say it was.

Since we know it is possible to be filled with the fullness of God, we must then be compelled to find out how we can be filled with this fullness. The answer is found in the person of Jesus.

Beware lest anyone cheat you through philosophy

and empty deceit, according to the tradition of men,
according to the basic principles of the world,
and not according to Christ. For in Him dwells all the fullness of
the Godhead bodily; and you are complete in Him,
who is the head of all principality and power.
Colossians 2:8-10

And He put all things under His feet, and gave Him
to be head over all things to the church, which is His body,
the fullness of Him who fills all in all.
Ephesians 1:22-23

And raised us up together, and made us sit together
in the heavenly places in Christ Jesus.
Ephesians 2:6

Christ is the fullness of the Godhead in bodily form. He has made us His body. The way we can experience the fullness of God is to sit with Christ Jesus in heavenly places. However, we as the church tend to live way below where we should be living.

We are on Day Twenty-One of a fast. Our faith should be at an all-time high. We should be ready to soar with God. We ought to be at a place where we believe that the Lord has every great thing for us, and we are confident to ask for it. We should believe that there is no hindrance to being filled with all the fullness of God. We should desire it, not so we can boast, but so God can be glorified in the earth.

The Lord is ready to bless us; favor us; extend great grace to us; overflow us; direct us; lead us; guide us; and perform signs, wonders, and miracles through us, and we have to get to a place where we realize that we are seated with Christ in heavenly places to see all of these things come to pass. When we realize our position, we will have confidence that we can be filled with the fullness of God.

Just think about the fullness of God. It means we can love as God loves. It means it would be possible for us to lay our hands on the sick and they would recover. It means we could raise the dead to life. It is possible. Our faith has to reach out to a place where we believe God has great things for us, and we are willing to ask for it. To get to this place we have to repent for any small thinking. We've all been guilty of it. We've all been guilty of trying to predict God's pattern. We've all tried to strategize the way He can accomplish the thing we are asking for. Oftentimes, He does not follow the pattern we thought of at all. It's because our thinking was too small.

We have to know that five loaves and two fish is more than enough to feed thousands. We have to know that throwing our nets on the other side of the boat will bring the massive catch we have been working so hard for. We have to think big enough to ask God to show up big in our situation and not limit Him to our capabilities. We must get out of the mindset that things have to be certain way. His ways are higher than our ways; His thoughts are higher than our thoughts. To walk in overflow, we must position ourselves to receive the fullness of God. I promise you, it will be more than you ever thought it could be.

When our church was at our previous campus, we were in desperate need of a new building. Everything was too small. We were doing three services every Sunday morning. We were doing the best we could with what we had. Meanwhile, we kept trying to get plans and break new ground for larger facilities. However, there always seemed to be a block on it. It seemed like it wasn't the will of God. Whatever it was, we couldn't figure it out.

What I did know was what I had heard from God. He had told me that when we walked into our new building, it would be paid for. That's all I had. I stood in front of our church for two years and told them we would get a new building, and that on day one, it would be debt-free. However, I kept thinking it would be a new building we would build, on the property we already occupied. This is why it was so frustrating. I was taking God's word, but putting it into my plan. The word was too big for my plan. It actually felt like I was fighting against God. Finally, the board and I took a step back from it and prayed.

After this, we became aware of a property with a building already on it. After about a month of prayer, we sensed that this was the will of God, and we began to talk with the bank, who owned the property, and within a month, we closed on the property. We were able to pay cash for the property and for the renovations it needed. That first day we walked into that completed building to worship, we walked in debt-free.

Until my way lined up with God's way, I was not going to see His word fulfilled. We have to get out of the rut of trying to constantly figure it out and let God speak. It's up to me to believe when God says it, then wait for Him to perform it. This is how we walk in fullness. He is able to do more than we can ask *or think*! We need to position ourselves to believe and receive, and walk in His fullness by embracing His way.

I feel in my spirit that many who are reading this have been holding onto a word from God for a long time. You know you have a word from God, but it seems like nothing is lining up. Perhaps the issue has been that you are simultaneously holding onto His word and your way. Those two things will never line up. If this is the case with you, I want you to pray, "God, I have Your word. Will you please show me Your way? However, you choose to do it, I yield to You and embrace Your way. I want to see it come to pass, and I want to experience Your fullness."

This is overflow. We don't need to know how, when, where, or with whom it's going to happen. We just need to trust God to bring it about for our good and His glory. It's time to throw our plans away. When we do this, we will see miracles.

Let's pray together . . .

Father, in the name of Jesus, I ask You to fill me today with all of the fullness of God. I ask You to forgive me for any and all small thinking and believing. I ask You to do exceeding abundantly above all I can ask, or even think.

I thank You, Lord, for the overflow. I give You praise that this overflow will never cease in my life, but that it will grow each and every day. I ask all of these things in Jesus' name. Amen.

ASK YOURSELF

- What are some ways I can expand beyond small thinking?

- What areas of my life are creating frustration?

- Am I frustrated because my ways are not lining up with God's words?

- How can I release my ambitions to embrace the fullness of God?

HEAVENLY
FIRE

HEAVENLY FIRE
DAY TWENTY-TWO AND BEYOND

There is a very good chance that you picked up this devotional and began this fast over three weeks ago because you were tired of the mundane. You were likely sick of the usual, and desired more of God. You were tired of living below what He had for you and decided you wanted more, even if it meant something as radical as what you've just done. I say this, because this is how it was with our ministry.

When we went into this, we wanted two things: Spiritual Restoration and Heavenly Fire. What we did not know was how it would look. When we cried out for the fire, God sent it to us, and it has not ceased to burn. We have been forever marked by His presence. We have been forever marked by the fire.

So many churches these days seem to be moving away from the power and demonstration of the Holy Spirit. They have even made efforts to do away with the moving of the Spirit. What has been forgotten is the fact that it is the glory that shows us that we need to bow. When the people of Israel saw the fire that had come down from heaven, they bowed their faces to the ground. Oh how desperate we are, and how desperately we need fresh fire!

When Solomon had finished praying, fire came down from heaven and consumed the burnt offering and the sacrifices; and the glory of the Lord filled the temple. And the priests could not enter the house of the Lord, because the glory of the Lord had filled the Lord's house. When all the children of Israel saw how the fire came down, and the glory of the Lord on the temple, they bowed their faces to the ground on the pavement, and worshiped and praised the Lord, saying:

"For He is good,
For His mercy endures forever."
2 Chronicles 7:1-3

When the Day of Pentecost had fully come,
they were all with one accord in one place.
And suddenly there came a sound from heaven,
as of a rushing mighty wind, and it filled the whole house
where they were sitting. Then there appeared to them
divided tongues, as of fire, and one sat upon each of them.
And they were all filled with the Holy Spirit and began
to speak with other tongues,
as the Spirit gave them utterance.
Acts 2:1-4

I know you have just gone through twenty-one days of emptying yourself of yourself, being filled with the Holy Spirit, and walking into overflow, and you might be wondering why we added more. Isn't it enough that we are no longer consumed with ourselves? Isn't it enough that we have been baptized in the Holy Spirit? Isn't it enough that we are focused on walking in daily overflow?

As we walked through this process, we found that it exposed our need for a fresh, daily encounter with the fire of God. We became tired of the things that brought complacency, unfaithfulness, prayerlessness, apathy, and lack of devotion to God. We grew tired of listening to messages, always thinking they were for someone else. We needed the fire of God to burn so powerfully in us that even if we were the only ones, we wanted, needed, for it to change us.

We need the fire to fall on us until we aren't the same anymore. We need the fire to fall on us until we lay our addictions, perversions, and sins down. We need the fire to fall on us until peace returns, marriages are restored, and our prodigals come home. We need the fire to fall on us until our family, friends, classmates, co-workers, and neighbors are saved.

Say this with me . . . *FIRE, FALL ON ME!*

When is the last time you felt the fire of God? When is the last time you felt His presence so powerfully that you wept in His presence? Are you as bold a witness now as you have ever been? Are you winning souls for the Kingdom of God? Do you want more fire?

We need fire to fall on us until our lives represent a fire-filled life. We need fire to fall on us until we stop slipping back into who we used to be. We need fire to fall on us until our marriages and families aren't messed up anymore. We need fire falling on us until we stop complaining about serving in the Kingdom of God, until we realize it is a privilege to serve in His Kingdom. We need the fire to fall on us until we can pray, read the Word, and hear from heaven consistently. We need fire to fall on us until we can love and forgive. We need fresh fire!

We need heavenly fire to transform our lives. We need fire so we can stop looking around and start looking within. We need fire to let go of our secret sins. We need fire so we can lay down self-righteous, religious spirits. We need fire to let go of the past that haunts us. We need fire to lay down the pain and regrets of yesterday. We need fire to get rid of the devils that have attempted to hinder us from walking in the glory and power of the Holy Spirit.

God has always been a consuming fire. He didn't wait to become a fire until the New Testament. All throughout scripture, we see God as a fire.

Moses was in the desert, running from God, and running from the call on his life, when he met God as a fire.

And the Angel of the Lord appeared to him in a flame
of fire from the midst of a bush. So he looked,
and behold, the bush was burning with fire,
but the bush was not consumed. Then Moses said,
"I will now turn aside and see this great sight,
why the bush does not burn."

So when the Lord saw that he turned aside to look,
God called to him from the midst of the bush and said,
"Moses, Moses!"

And he said, "Here I am."
Then He said, "Do not draw near this place.
Take your sandals off your feet, for the place where
you stand is holy ground."
Exodus 3:2-5

God showed up again, as fire, to guide His people in the wilderness.

And the Lord went before them by day in a pillar
of cloud to lead the way, and by night in a pillar of fire
to give them light, so as to go by day and night.
Exodus 13:21

God showed His people that the fire had to constantly be burning.

"Command Aaron and his sons, saying,
'This is the law of the burnt offering:
The burnt offering shall be on the hearth upon the altar
all night until morning, and the fire of the altar shall be kept
burning on it. And the priest shall put on his linen garment,
and his linen trousers he shall put on his body,
and take up the ashes of the burnt offering which the fire
has consumed on the altar, and he shall put them
beside the altar. Then he shall take off his garments,
put on other garments, and carry the ashes outside
the camp to a clean place. And the fire on the altar
shall be kept burning on it; it shall not be put out.
And the priest shall burn wood on it every morning,
and lay the burnt offering in order on it;
and he shall burn on it the fat of the peace offerings.
A fire shall always be burning on the altar;
it shall never go out.'"
Leviticus 6:9-13

In the house of God, the only fire that could be used was the fire sent by God. Mankind could not create the fire. Everything had to come from holy fire.

Then Nadab and Abihu, the sons of Aaron,
each took his censer and put fire in it,
put incense on it, and offered profane fire before the Lord,
which He had not commanded them.
So fire went out from the Lord and devoured them,
and they died before the Lord.
Leviticus 10:1-2

God used fire to define Himself to us. He wants us all to Himself.

For the Lord your God is a consuming fire, a jealous God.
Deuteronomy 4:24

Before God would let the fire go out, he called a prophet that would speak to the nation of Israel.

Now the boy Samuel ministered to the Lord before Eli.
And the word of the Lord was rare in those days; there was no
widespread revelation. And it came to pass at that time,
while Eli was lying down in his place, and when his eyes had
begun to grow so dim that he could not see, and before the lamp
of God went out in the tabernacle of the Lord where the ark of
God was, and while Samuel was lying down,
that the Lord called Samuel. And he answered, "Here I am!"
1 Samuel 3:1-4

When Baal-worship had overtaken God's people, He sent His prophet Elijah to the top of Mount Carmel to prove who was indeed God and who was false. After the prophets of Baal spent all day begging their god to send fire, Elijah stepped up.

And it came to pass, at the time of the offering of the evening sacrifice, that Elijah the prophet came near and said, "Lord God of Abraham, Isaac, and Israel, let it be known this day that You are God in Israel and I am Your servant, and that I have done all these things at Your word. Hear me, O Lord, hear me, that this people may know that You are the Lord God, and that You have turned their hearts back to You again."

Then the fire of the Lord fell and consumed the burnt sacrifice,
and the wood and the stones and the dust,
and it licked up the water that was in the trench.
Now when all the people saw it, they fell on their faces;
and they said, "The Lord, He is God! The Lord, He is God!"
1 Kings 18:36-39

As we move into the New Testament, it does not take very long before we begin to see God as a fire again.

"I indeed baptize you with water unto repentance,
but He who is coming after me is mightier than I,
whose sandals I am not worthy to carry.
He will baptize you with the Holy Spirit and fire."
Matthew 3:11

We can't sit in our complacency any longer. We can't stay as we are and allow our inaction to say *no* to the calling of God to enter the fire. We can't stay in our seats while the altar is open with a fire ready. To say *no* to fire is to say no to Jesus.

Jesus' desire was to send the fire, even though He knew it would cause unrest and division. He knows fire always brings separation.

"I came to send fire on the earth,
and how I wish it were already kindled!
But I have a baptism to be baptized with,
and how distressed I am till it is accomplished!
Do you suppose that I came to give peace on earth?
I tell you, not at all, but rather division.
For from now on five in one house will be divided:
three against two, and two against three.
Father will be divided against son and son against father,
mother against daughter and daughter against mother,
mother-in-law against her daughter-in-law and
daughter-in-law against her mother-in-law."
Luke 12:49-53

Jesus didn't ask His disciples to wait in Jerusalem for the promised Holy Spirit; He commanded them to. When they asked Him whether this would be the time He restored the Kingdom of God in the earth, He let them know that He wanted to restore the Kingdom in them.

And being assembled together with them,
He commanded them not to depart from Jerusalem,
but to wait for the Promise of the Father, "which,"
He said, "you have heard from Me; for John truly
baptized with water, but you shall be baptized
with the Holy Spirit not many days from now."
Therefore, when they had come together,
they asked Him, saying, "Lord, will You at this time restore
the kingdom to Israel?" And He said to them,
"It is not for you to know times or seasons which the
Father has put in His own authority.
But you shall receive power when the

Holy Spirit has come upon you;
and you shall be witnesses to Me in Jerusalem,
and in all Judea and Samaria,
and to the end of the earth."
Acts 1:4-8

We have been given a power from on high. This is a power to face down death, heal the sick, proclaim Jesus to the lost, shift atmospheres, and shake the kingdom of darkness. He didn't desire a fire so we can keep it right where we were, but so that we would be compelled to take it to our homes, jobs, schools, cities, regions, states, nations, and to the ends of the earth. God is not about relegating His fire to buildings. He wants to put it in us, His temples. The fire from heaven that descended on tabernacles and temples now falls on us.

When Jesus came to this earth, He came for the purpose of being mocked, rejected, beaten, tortured, and executed on the cross, to atone for the sins of mankind. After being taken down from the cross, His dead body was placed in a tomb. He descended into hell and took back the authority from the principalities and rulers of wickedness. He paraded a defeated Satan openly before them all. He snatched the keys of death, hell, and the grave. He released the captive saints and brought them before the throne of His Father, where He brought the atoning blood once and for all. He was resurrected on the third day. He showed Himself alive for forty days, proving to the haters, doubters, and deniers that He was alive, just as He had promised. After instructing His disciples to wait in Jerusalem for the promised Holy Spirit, He ascended into heaven, letting them know that they would do even greater works than He did. When He returned to the Father, He prayed that He would send the Holy Spirit on those who were seeking Him.

When the Day of Pentecost had fully come, they were all gathered in one accord. There was no doubting or division. There came a sound like a mighty rushing wind, and they were all filled with the Holy Spirit. The fire, in the form of divided tongues, descended on them and sat on top of each one. He has always been the God of fire, and He will always be the God of fire.

As soon as this fire came, Simon Peter stood up and began to preach his first sermon. As he began to explain to the people what they were hearing and seeing, he had this to say about the Holy Spirit and fire:

> *For the promise is to you and to your children,*
> *and to all who are afar off, as many as the*
> *Lord our God will call.*
> *Acts 2:39*

On the day I was born again, I was at the altar for over two hours. I didn't come to Jesus because I wanted my house back or my car back. I came to Jesus because I was a sinner. I had sinned against a holy God, and I deserved hell. When I realized how much my sin had hurt Him, it broke me. When I realized how much my sin had cost Him, it broke me. I wept before the Lord.

As glorious as it was, the next week, when I was baptized in the Holy Spirit, it was like a hundred times that. The previous week, I had struggled so hard to stay in the place I had been at the altar. However, when the power came, something reverberated out of me that I had never experienced. The God of heaven had come and made His home in me. I wish I could tell you that the one time was all it took, but I've found that every day I wake up, I need that fire to fall on me again. Every morning, I have to ask, "God, will you fill this vessel again?" Every morning, I ask Him to show up and pour fresh fire again. I can't live off yesterday's fire.

Many believers live with destruction because they are trying to live off yesterday's fire. We serve a God that desires to pour fresh fire on us every day. We can live a life that is no longer plagued by secret and habitual sins. Our marriages and families can be healed. We just need fresh fire from heaven. The world can't give it to us. And when we have it, the world can't take it from us.

If you need to renew your commitment to God, don't wait. Do it now. If you need fresh fire, ask for it now. Pray and seek God. Repent if you need to. You're going to get your passion back. You're going to get your fire back. You're going to dream again.

Father, in the name of Jesus, change me again with Your Holy Fire!

ASK YOURSELF

- Will I continue to desire the fire of God to the point that I refuse to watch, listen to, or do things that will hinder it?

- What personal price am I willing to pay to have heavenly fire burn in my life?

- What way do I presently feel God's fire burning within me?

NOW WHAT?

DAY TWENTY-TWO AND BEYOND

NOW WHAT?

*Now the Lord said to Samuel, "How long will you mourn for
Saul, seeing I have rejected him from reigning over Israel?
Fill your horn with oil, and go; I am sending you to Jesse the
Bethlehemite. For I have provided Myself a king among his sons."*

And Samuel said, "How can I go? If Saul hears it, he will kill me."

*But the Lord said, "Take a heifer with you, and say, '
I have come to sacrifice to the Lord.' Then invite Jesse to
the sacrifice, and I will show you what you shall do; you shall
anoint for Me the one I name to you."*

*So Samuel did what the Lord said, and went to Bethlehem.
And the elders of the town trembled at his coming, and said,
"Do you come peaceably?"*

*And he said, "Peaceably; I have come to sacrifice to the Lord.
Sanctify yourselves, and come with me to the sacrifice."
Then he consecrated Jesse and his sons,
and invited them to the sacrifice.*

*So it was, when they came, that he looked at Eliab and said,
"Surely the Lord's anointed is before Him!"*

*But the Lord said to Samuel, "Do not look at his appearance
or at his physical stature, because I have refused him.
For the Lord does not see as man sees; for man looks at the outward appearance, but the Lord looks at the heart."*

*So Jesse called Abinadab, and made him pass before Samuel.
And he said, "Neither has the Lord chosen this one."
Then Jesse made Shammah pass by. And he said,
"Neither has the Lord chosen this one." Thus Jesse made seven
of his sons pass before Samuel. And Samuel said to Jesse,
"The Lord has not chosen these." And Samuel said to Jesse,
"Are all the young men here?" Then he said,
"There remains yet the youngest, and there he is,
keeping the sheep."*

*And Samuel said to Jesse, "Send and bring him.
For we will not sit down till he comes here." So he sent and
brought him in. Now he was ruddy, with bright eyes,
and good-looking. And the Lord said, "Arise, anoint him;
for this is the one!" Then Samuel took the horn of oil and
anointed him in the midst of his brothers; and the Spirit
of the Lord came upon David from that day forward.
So Samuel arose and went to Ramah.*

*But the Spirit of the Lord departed from Saul,
and a distressing spirit from the Lord troubled him.
1 Samuel 16:1-14*

I believe this is a prophetic word for your life today. As you
receive this, I believe that it will impact you to the depths of your
very soul. As you respond to it, the anointing of the Holy Spirit
will meet you in your response and do something in your life.

No matter how many times you try to resuscitate something, if God intends for it to die, it will die. This is why we must be led by the Spirit, so we can live where God intends for life to exist. This is what was happening with the prophet Samuel. Saul's kingdom was dead, because God intended for it to be dead.

When the prophet stood before David's eldest brother, Eliab, he saw strength and stature, but God made sure to let Samuel know that He had not merely not chosen him, but that He had looked at his heart and had refused him. God cared nothing for strength and stature; He was looking for the right heart. Seven sons, representing seven different things, passed before the prophet. All were rejected. The Lord saw the humility of David and knew that was something He could use.

Lou Engle said, "Revelation demands participation."

We have just finished twenty-one days of prayer and fasting. We spent three full weeks seeking God, but *now what?*

If our experience with God is just an event, we will never change a nation. If it is merely a three-week occurrence, we will never shift regions, generations, schools, and governments. If our experience is just for twenty-one days, we did it in vain. However, if this experience has changed our lifestyle, now the power of God will fall, His Spirit will spread, and people will be transformed by the gospel.

Now what?

Just as it was with David, God does not have to ask anyone's opinion about whom He anoints and promotes. If God has chosen someone, there is no person, no angel, nor demon that can stop Him. He will pick people and He will raise them up for His glory. We don't need big titles or big stages to get the attention of our big God. It doesn't matter how low we feel, or how hidden we are, God knows how to find us. He sees in me what man can't give to me. No matter what it is buried under, God can still see it. My faith in what He has given me now can open the door for what He chooses to give me tomorrow.

The prophet has come from Ramah to Bethlehem, looking for someone to anoint as king over Israel. He is impressed with the selection in front of Him, because he is comparing them to what Israel already had. Saul looks the part of a king. God, however, is doing a new thing.

Samuel takes the horn, filled with oil, and pours it over David, and the Spirit of the Lord comes upon David, from that day forward. The runt of the family, the one many scholars believe was conceived illegitimately, was chosen by God. In front of his father and his brothers, he is dripping with the oil signifying his anointing as the king of Israel. Now what?

During the twenty-one days of prayer and fasting, many of us got our passion back. Many got their fire back. Some stepped back into their call. Marriages were healed. Mighty things were done in finances. Ministry has taken on a whole new level. We are ready to run. We are ready to fight. Now what? Will we leave the twenty-one days where we left them, or will we move forward in the plan and the will of God? The Holy Spirit told me to ask you, *Now what?*

Now what?

Just as the prophet anointed David, and the Spirit of the Lord came upon him, the Lord has poured a new anointing on you in this time of fasting and prayer. You've been given this anointing to walk in, not sit in. We can no longer be anointed and sit on it. God is asking you to walk in this anointing. We can either step out, or sit here and always wonder what could have happened. What are you going to do with this anointing now? I'm talking to the youngest and the oldest. I'm talking to the new Christian and the mature Christian. I'm talking to the high-ranking minister and the one who doesn't even have a place of ministry yet. Will you walk in it, or sit in it?

From the time David was anointed to the time he ascended the throne of Israel was fourteen years. Fourteen years of wanting to do something, but not being able to. Fourteen years of people wondering when it was going to happen. Fourteen years of leading armies to victory, but not being able to lead the nation. However, it was also fourteen years of not sitting on the anointing, but of walking it out. He found the thing he was allowed to put his hands to, and did it with all of his might.

David had a mindset many of us need to adopt. Just because the palace was filled didn't mean he would sit still. Just because Saul was in his seat didn't mean he would sit in defeat. Just because he had not yet been appointed did not mean he was not anointed. He had an anointing and he stepped out into what he could do. He wasn't caught up in waiting for a position. He had already been empowered. When he walked in the power, the position opened.

People who are hungry for position are dangerous. They will kill, lie, cheat, and steal to get position. They will turn on people as fast as a rattlesnake. I'm always cautious of people who want position, even when I know they have power to do great things for the Kingdom. I'm wary of people who won't preach or pray until they've been given position. Saul wanted to maintain his position, and it made him dangerous.

In Acts 1, Jesus did not tell them to go to Jerusalem and wait on a position. The Pharisees and Sadducees were not going to relinquish their positions. Instead, He instructed them to go and wait on the power. This power would cause them to be witnesses in Jerusalem, Judea, Samaria, and to the ends of the earth.

What we received over these twenty-one days of fasting and prayer was not position—it was power. Now we must walk in the power of the Holy Spirit and fulfill the call of God on our lives. We are no longer looking for the limelight. We are looking for daylight to go shine in a dark world.

Now what?

Our time of prayer and fasting is over. We have received from the Lord what we asked of Him. Have we done what He has asked us to do, or are we still sitting on it? Some of us prayed that God would make us a better witness. Have we witnessed yet? Some asked the Lord to help them be forgiving and loving. Have you forgiven whom you've needed to forgive yet?

God is confronting us at the core of who we are. He's challenging us with the fact that He has given us what we have asked for. *Now what* are we going to do with it? We've been given an anointing to do great things. *Now what?* I know you may not necessarily feel different right now, but you are different. *Now what?*

In Ezekiel 47, God shows the prophet water flowing from the doors of the temple and healing the stagnant waters of the sea. When the prophet first stepped into the water, it was up to his ankles. Still, he kept walking. The more he walked, the deeper it got. He didn't stop at ankle-deep, or waist-deep. He didn't stop at neck-deep. He finally made it to a place where it was so deep he could only swim in it. This is representative of the anointing that has come upon you and me in this season of seeking God. If we will just keep walking in it, God has an overwhelming anointing that will heal the stagnant parts of our lives. It will be so deep we can only flow with the move of God. Keep walking—it will get deeper.

We don't all have the same giftings, callings, opportunities, or spheres of influence, but we all have a mandate from God to operate in what we are given. It's not the time to sit it out. It's time to walk it out. He will perform signs and wonders through us all, if we will only walk it out.

Now what?

We have unclean and distressing spirits to drive out, not drive with. For too long we have ministered with unclean spirits, instead of casting them out.

After the anointing of David, an evil spirit came to torment Saul. Nothing they did could help Saul. He could get no peace. He could not sleep. Finally, someone said there's a man of God who can play the harp under such anointing that it drives away the evil spirits. Saul told them to get this man to him. David came before the king, harp in hand, and began to play, and the anointing caused the distressing spirits to leave.

We have been given an anointing. When we minister, the distressing spirits have to leave, because of the God in us. They have occupied space in our lives illegally. They have no business in our homes, our lives, and our ministries. We're not trying to coexist with these spirits. We're not attempting to minister with them, or in spite of them. We are taking authority, and making them go. We give them no room to operate. We have an anointing that drives them out.

God has released an anointing on you. Whether you are playing a harp, keeping kids, preaching the Word, opening doors, running sound, leading worship, or cleaning the floors, you have been given an anointing to drive out spirits. So, quit playing with them. Drive them out. These spirits have hindered long enough. They've kept people sick, bound, addicted, perverted, racist, self-righteous, and impoverished long enough. It's time we serve an eviction notice to these spirits.

And He [Jesus] said to them,
"Go into all the world and preach the gospel to every creature.
He who believes and is baptized will be saved;
but he who does not believe will be condemned.
And these signs will follow those who believe:
In My name they will cast out demons;
they will speak with new tongues;
they will take up serpents;
and if they drink anything deadly,
it will by no means hurt them;
they will lay hands on the sick, and they will recover."
Mark 16:15-18

In the name of Jesus, I stand in agreement with you today, and we drive out the spirits of complacency and apathy. We drive out the spirits of confusion and distress. We drive out the spirits of infirmity, sickness, and disease. We evict the spirits of quarrel, enmity, and division. We drive out every spirit of delay. We command the spirits of deception, lies, perversion, and immorality to go now. Spirit of divorce, you must leave. Every spirit that has been hidden is now revealed and evicted. Leave our homes, families, and ministries. We evict you and declare we will never be bound by these again.

In their place, we release overflow in the spirit realm and the natural realm. We release power, purpose, clarity, peace, healing, unity, prosperity, truth, holiness, righteousness, togetherness, and agreement. Where there has been restriction, we release *Rehoboth*, a wide place. Everything that was taken must be restored at least seven-fold. We serve notice on the lying serpent of hell that, starting now, we are walking in the overflow of heavenly fire!

God has anointed you to pull down strongholds, to defeat giants, and to command spirits. You have an anointing to call prodigals home. Right now, just lift your hands and begin to pray. Pray in the Spirit and pray with your understanding. Serve notice on the forces of darkness. They no longer have a place in your life.

Take the next two minutes and begin to declare aloud what the Holy Spirit has put into your heart to declare. Bind up the works of the enemy in your life, and cast them out, in Jesus' name. Evict every unclean, hindering spirit. Command them to loose you, and let you go. Release the prophetic over your life.

Now what?

We have giants to slay, not to obey.

David entered the Valley of Elah, at Sochoh, in obedience. He had been asked by his father, Jesse, to check on the state of his brothers and to deliver cheese to their commanding officers. He went in obedience to deliver cheese, but in an anointing to deliver a nation.

When David showed up, the giant began to shout. Why? Because the anointing will always make the giant shout. When the giant shouted, the anointing caused David to step up. Why? Because the anointing will always push us to the forefront of the battle. David quickly realized that his responsibility was to obey his father, but his anointing was to slay a giant. He began to understand that his past battles with the lion and the bear were preparation for his present war. Now he knew why what should have killed him, didn't.

What was designed to kill you didn't kill you. You are anointed to slay giants. Your past lions had loud roars. Your past bears loomed large. But they couldn't take you out. It's the season for overflow, and you're still here. God kept David, and He kept you, because you have an anointing to wipe out giants.

Now you know why God wouldn't let you quit. When you wanted to throw in the towel, you just couldn't. You were designed for this moment. You won't always be where you are. You won't always be facing what you're facing this day. This is a prophetic moment for you. You've had twenty-one days with you and the Spirit. You're empowered. You're prepared. You're anointed, appointed, and called. It doesn't matter who is sitting in the palace. It's time to walk in your assignment. The Holy Spirit has put the ball back in your court, and He's asking you this question:

Now what?

Let's pray together . . .

Father, in the name of Jesus, I come before You humbly. I ask today that a mighty anointing would fall upon me, like never before. I ask that my heart and my mind would be activated, stirred, electrified, and charged with Your Spirit. Let there be a fire that hits my life, where I would no longer be found guilty of doing nothing. Instead, let me be found guilty of advancing Your Kingdom, of preaching Your gospel, of loving my enemies, of giving until it hurts, of walking in Your truth, of being separated by the anointing of the Holy Spirit.

Look upon my availability, and not my ability, and do through me what only You can do. Let Your perfect will be done on earth as it is in heaven. Use me to transform lives, I pray, in Jesus' name. Amen.

ASK YOURSELF

- Am I seeking and striving to gain or keep position, or am I walking in the anointing I've been given to carry out the work of the Lord?

- Have I stopped where my feet can still touch the bottom of the river, or am I pushing forward to waters that can carry me?

- Am I avoiding, or even worse, obeying giants, or am I using the anointing upon me to slay them?

CPSIA information can be obtained
at www.ICGtesting.com
Printed in the USA
JSHW011225160120
3632JS00001B/6